W9-COH-582

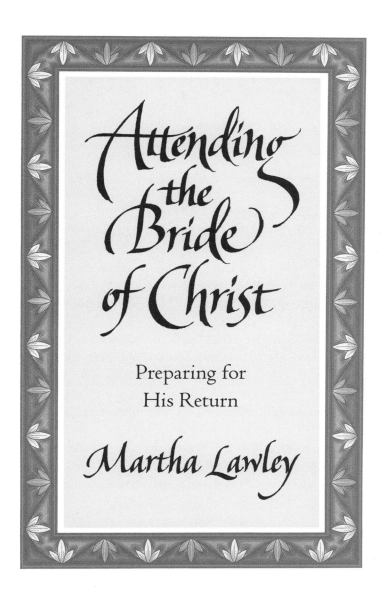

Attending the Bride of Christ

Preparing for
His Return

Martha Lawley

LifeWay Press®
Nashville, Tennessee

Published by LifeWay Press®
Third printing July 2010
©2005 Martha Lawley

No part of this book may be reproduced or transmitted in any form or by any means, electronic or mechanical, including photocopying and recording, or by any information storage or retrieval system, except as may be expressly permitted in writing by the publisher. Requests for permission should be addressed in writing to LifeWay Press® ; One LifeWay Plaza; Nashville, TN 37234-0175.

ISBN: 1-4158-2091-0

Dewey Decimal Classification Number: 262.7

Subject Headings: WOMEN–RELIGIOUS LIFE\ CHURCH\ MARRIAGE CUSTOMS AND RITES

Unless otherwise indicated, Scripture quotations are from the Holy Bible, New International Version, copyright © 1973, 1978, 1984 by International Bible Society.

Scripture quotations identified HCSB are from The Holman Christian Standard Bible®, © Copyright 2001 Holman Bible Publishers, Nashville, TN. Used by permission.

Scripture quotations identified KJV are from the King James Version.

Scripture quotations identified NASB are from The New American Standard Bible, Copyright © 1960, 1962, 1963, 1968, 1971, 1972, 1973, 1975, 1977, 1995 by the Lockman Foundation. Used by permission. (*www.lockman.org*)

To order additional copies of this resource, write to LifeWay Church Resources Customer Service; One LifeWay Plaza; Nashville, TN 37234-0013; fax (615) 251-5933; PHONE (800)458-2772; order online at *www.lifeway.com;* e-mail *orderentry@lifeway.com;* or visit the LifeWay Christian Store serving you.

Printed in the United States of America

Leadership and Adult Publishing
LifeWay Church Resources
One LifeWay Plaza
Nashville, TN 37234-0175

Contents

Week 1

A Picture of Relationship

6

Week 2

Past Reflections of the Future

28

Week 3

The Divine Partnership

48

Week 4

Ornaments of Grace

70

Week 5

Messages from the Bridegroom

92

Week 6

The Bridegrooms Return

116

About the Author

After graduating from Baylor Law School, Martha Lawley began her legal career in Houston, Texas, where she specialized in business litigation. While in Houston she met and married the love of her life, Roger Lawley. Martha continued to practice law until 1994, when God called her family to Utah. For the next five years Martha was blessed to be a full-time wife and mother as well as serving in her home church. Then, in late 1999, God called Martha to be the Women's Consultant for the Utah-Idaho Southern Baptist Convention where she served until her family relocated to northern Wyoming.

Martha has been blessed with many opportunities to lead women's conferences and retreats nationwide. God has given her a passion for discipleship and called her to minister to women. Her holistic approach to ministry emphasizes the importance of women being involved in each of the core spiritual disciplines of Bible study, in prayer, in worship, in using spiritual gifts in service, and in personal evangelism.

Martha also serves as a women's ministry multiplier for LifeWay Church Resources. She contributed to the women's leadership book, *Transformed Lives: Taking Women's Ministry to the Next Level*, published by LifeWay Press®, and has written articles for LifeWay's Women's Ministry Web page.

Martha attends First Southern Baptist Church of Worland, Wyoming, where she and Roger teach a singles Sunday School class. She also serves her home church as a Bible study leader and women's ministry team member. Martha and Roger have three wonderful children, a fabulous son-in-law, and a precious new grandson.

For more information on Martha's ministry, visit *www.marthalawley.com*.

Introduction

Today's church faces many challenges. In fact, some say it is a dying institution no longer relevant to the culture. I believe, however, that God designed the church with a specific purpose that is both eternal and unchanging. He reserved a special purpose for each believer that is discovered, developed, and ultimately fulfilled through the church body. But apart from grasping the certainty of Christ's imminent return, we cannot fully understand God's divine purposes.

My family went to church every time the doors were open. Considering all those Sundays, Wednesdays, and special evenings spent in pews, you might think I figured out what church is all about early on. But only as time passed did I begin to realize how little I really understood about church as described in the Bible.

For years I defined church based on my experiences with it rather than what God's Word says about it. As a result, I developed misconceptions about church that left me frustrated. But as God began to expose these fallacies, He filled me with a desire to know more about His perspective on church. The more I learned about church from God's Word, the better I understood its importance and the vital significance of each believer's involvement within it. Over time, I came to realize that God designed our relationship with Christ to be personal and shared— a partnership that cannot be separated from His church. This profound spiritual truth opened the way for me to hear God speak to me about my relationship with the church. Even today He uses those insights to change my attitudes and actions towards her.

Scripture portrays Christ as the divine bridegroom and the church as His bride—an image providing rich and important spiritual lessons. During the next six weeks we will embark on an exciting quest, pulling back the veil of time to catch a deeper glimpse into the God-given pattern of relationship between Christ and His bride. How I hope this study will encourage us to step outside our usual ways of thinking about the church, challenging us to change our actions toward her.

You don't need to be married to participate in this study. No matter your marriage status, *Attending the Bride of Christ* is designed to help you better understand God's plan for the church and your part in preparing for Christ's return. I pray God will use this study to encourage you to fully accept His gracious invitation to serve the bride of Christ by becoming a devoted and involved member of your local church body. I pray also that each of us will learn to truly treasure the divine privilege of attending Christ's bride.

Friend, I wish I could be with you during these next weeks so we could learn from one another! But even in my physical absence, my prayers are with you! Please take the time to participate in all of the learning activities provided; each is designed to assist you in applying what God is teaching you. Remember, if all we do during a study is gain more knowledge, we accomplish very little of eternal value. Commit to more than simply learning about attending the bride. Allow the Lord to radically transform you and your relationship with His church, *His* bride! You'll be glad you did.

Study
Week #1
Meeting 1 & 2

1

A Picture of Relationship

I'VE ALWAYS LOVED THE FIRST WORDS OF SCRIPTURE: "IN THE BEGINNING GOD ... " What simple but profound words! In the beginning God was. In the beginning He created. In the beginning He initiated a loving relationship with us, and God will perfect that relationship through the process of our transformation.

When my children were young, they loved to hear the story of my courtship with my husband, Roger. They wanted to know all the details. How did our relationship begin? How did we know we loved one another? How did Roger propose? Hearing how our family started seemed to give them a sense of security and belonging. It also served to remind Roger and me that God's plans for us were bigger than we realized.

Our study opens with the love story between Christ and the church. We'll discover how their relationship was initiated. We'll learn who chose the church as Christ's bride. Together we'll explore the beautiful relationship planned in the beginning and extending into eternity.

I'm so honored to share this exciting look at Scripture with you! It's my heart's prayer that you will find encouragement as well as a renewed sense of security and belonging as we explore this thrilling love story.

Day One
A Heavenly Perspective

Some filmmakers release a movie that tells the end of an epic story, then later release a prequel telling the story's beginning. Knowing how a story concludes makes seemingly unimportant events glow with significance. Characters and details I'd otherwise overlook take on new and exciting meaning because of what I know about the story's end.

The Bible tells the epic true story of God's love for His creation, revealing a glorious plan at work since the beginning of time. As the story unfolds, we discover history speeding steadily toward one central event–the wedding of the Lamb. With the stage set by thousands of years of redemptive history, the Book of Revelation describes this much-anticipated moment with touching detail.

By beginning at the end of the story, we can better understand both the Old and New Testament. Bible passages often overlooked or misunderstood become more meaningful when we know how the story–our story–ends.

With this is mind, let's begin by fast-forwarding to the end–John's revelation of future events.

Search the Scripture

Read Revelation 1:1-3. To whom do the words in verse 3 apply?
- ○ just early believers
- ○ pastors and church leaders only
- ● all who take to heart the message

Read Revelation 19:6-9. What event does it describe?

The marriage of the Lamb has come + His bride has made herself ready - The wedding of The Lamb.

What does this passage tell us about the church's preparation for the celebration (vv. 7-8)?

Clothe Yourselves in righteousness righteous deeds

What do you think verse 9 means—that those invited to the marriage feast of the Lamb are blessed?

What God Says is right
Those invited + Believers + are righteous as they have Confessed Their Sins + accepted Christ as their Savior.

INDIVIDUAL TRUTHS

FIT TOGETHER LIKE INTERSECTNG PUZZLE PIECES.

Make It Personal

I don't understand many things in the Book of Revelation, but I do know the book sheds valuable light on our eternal future. God promises a special blessing to those who not only hear, but also "take to heart what is written in it" (Rev. 1:3). I believe that blessing includes a better understanding of both Scripture and present events.

Over the years I've asked myself one frustrating question after another trying to make sense of my circumstances. *Why is this happening? Why now? What am I supposed to do about it?* How I longed to know what God wanted from me! I searched the Scriptures for answers but still couldn't quite see the big picture. I needed God to help me see things from His viewpoint.

Over time I began to see how individual biblical truths fit together like intersecting puzzle pieces. God slowly revealed His kingdom perspective–His infinite plan–for the church and for each believer. I began to grasp His plan for me.

Perhaps you, too, seek to understand and long to discover where you fit in God's big picture. I promise you do fit. God wants us to know the answers to these important questions, and He will help us if only we'll ask.

Have you ever wondered what God wants from you and how the church fits into that plan? ◉ yes ○ no

As we begin our journey together, let's establish a baseline to measure our progress.

On a sheet of paper answer or complete the following:
- What is your definition of church? *evangelism, worship + Praise body of believers*
- How did you form your personal beliefs and attitudes about church?
- How would you describe the purpose of church? *to teach the gospel*
- Briefly describe your understanding of God's plan for your life. — *Glorify God + Prepare for His Son's return from heaven to gather His church - believers*
- Describe your current local church involvement.

Seal your answers in an envelope and—here's the hard part—put the envelope away where you can find it during the last week of our study. *P take us to heaven*

Discover the Meaning

To understand God's perspective we need to grasp His divine time line. With that in mind, imagine God's kingdom calendar open like a huge daily planner. One day records a tiny infant King born in Bethlehem. Another day–the day of Pentecost–records the Holy Spirit falling like fire! Each past, present, and future event is an important part of God's master plan–an important part of His plan for us.

If we could flip ahead we would find an extraordinary entry penned by God's hand–on a date known only to Him. That event is the wedding of the Lamb! Heaven brims with excitement as saints and angels wait for that day, poised to burst forth with compulsory praise, expressive joy, and unparalleled celebration (Rev. 19).

Let's put the wedding of the Lamb in context with other major kingdom events. Read the following verses, placing them in their proper places on the chart:

- Acts 2:1-41
- Genesis 1:1
- Acts 1:9-11
- Matthew 1:22-23
- 1 Thessalonians 4:16-18
- Matthew 24:36

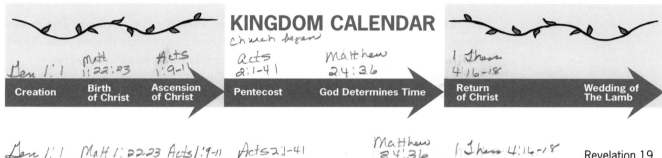

KINGDOM CALENDAR

Church began

Gen 1:1 — Matt 1:22:23 — Acts 1:9-11 — Acts 2:1-41

Matthew 24:36 — 1 Thess 4:16-18

| Creation | Birth of Christ | Ascension of Christ | Pentecost | God Determines Time | Return of Christ | Wedding of The Lamb |

Gen 1:1 MaH 1:22.23 Acts1:9-11 Acts 2:1-41   Matthew 24:36   1 Thess 4:16-18   Revelation 19

These Scriptures record only a few major events on God's kingdom calendar; we'd need stacks of paper to include them all. These particular events, however, provide the framework for our study and will help develop our kingdom perspective.

We'll occasionally refer to this illustration to position what we learn in its proper place on the kingdom calendar. In the meantime, remember that all heaven awaits the glorious wedding of the Lamb—an event to which we as Christians are invited. I pray God will grow our anticipation of that blessed day in the weeks ahead!

Day Two
A Powerful Illustration

I'm so thankful for my wonderful husband, Roger. Through our relationship God has blessed me beyond description. While I'm glad God appointed me to be a wife, I have single friends who are equally glad God has not appointed them to marriage.

As we explore the use of wedding imagery in the Bible, understand that this study is not about marriage; instead, it's about living God's will. The Lord frequently used the marriage relationship to teach us about Himself, His purposes, and His ways. But you don't have to be married to understand the beautiful spiritual truths illustrated by the biblical marriage experience.

Compare Jeremiah 2:1-2; Jeremiah 3:20; and Ezekiel 16:32. To what do each of these verses compare Israel? (Check all that apply.)

○ daughter   ● bride   ● adulterous woman   ● wife

How does God refer to Himself in Isaiah 54:5; Jeremiah 3:14; and Hosea 2:16?

husband, Maker, LORD of hosts, Redeemer, Holy One of Israel God of all the earth   Ishi — no longer Baali

Throughout the Old Testament, God declares Israel His bride or wife. This image taught the Israelites about their sacred relationship with their Creator (Isa. 61:10; 62:5) and described a coming, everlasting covenant relationship with Him.

What do Jeremiah 31:31-34 and Hosea 2:16-20 reveal about God's plan for future relationship with His people?

○ Through a business transaction, He will sell them to their enemies.
● Through covenant, He will take them as His bride.
○ Through discipline, He will punish them for their sins.

The bridal covenant illustration continues throughout the Old and New Testaments. Not only did Jesus often choose the marriage experience to teach about Himself and His relationship with His followers, but He ultimately fulfilled His Father's promise of a new covenant described in Jeremiah 31:31-33.

To whom is this new covenant relationship available (Rom. 1:16)?

Everyone who believes the gospel

Make It Personal

Why do you think God chose the marriage relationship to teach spiritual truth?

beauty, truth, love, devotion + loyalty respect, submission

union

to demonstrate the good and the unfaithful relationship our itimanus in the relationship — the Shepherd + the Sheep Spiritual Covenant   protection

For years I passed over the marriage imagery in Scripture, not considering its full meaning. Brides and grooms seemed more poetic than personal; "wedding feast" sounded like nothing more than an exaggerated reference to fellowship. Since I also lacked knowledge concerning Jewish tradition, I missed vital truths about my relationship with Christ and His relationship with the church. In retrospect, I think I missed much of the beauty behind salvation.

Discover the Meaning

The Bible uses many illustrations. As I learn more about gardening, I gain insight into God's role as gardener (John 15:1). Learning more about shepherding enriches my understanding of the 23rd Psalm. Not surprisingly, learning about the Jewish marriage experience enriches my understanding of Christ and the church. While some images are occasional illustrations, however, marriage may be the most sacred and central picture in Scripture.

My interest in Jewish tradition began years ago during conversations with my Jewish law partner, Roger Shoss. Roger is not only a highly competent corporate lawyer but also a sincere, practicing Jew. I was inspired as he shared how his grandparents fled Russia to escape persecution, and I became intrigued by his personal adherence to and love for the Jewish faith.

Hoping to better understand Judaism through our talks, I listened intently as he patiently responded to my countless questions. Our discussions gave me insight into the Jewish way of thinking and helped me see that Scripture was written from a Jewish mind-set. After all, God chose the Jews to be His covenant people, Jesus was a practicing Jew, and the early church was predominately Jewish.

What began as simple curiosity became a growing desire to know more about Jewish history and traditions. I could never have imagined how those insights would profoundly expand my understanding of God's Word.

MARRIAGE
MAY BE THE MOST
SACRED AND
CENTRAL PICTURE
IN SCRIPTURE.

Have you ever learned more about a certain custom or profession mentioned in the Bible with the result of enriching your understanding of Scripture? ○ yes ○ no **If so, explain.**

warrior, king, Pharoah, disciple
Shepherd, reaping wheat in Ruth & gleaning & Shearer of Sheep

During this first week we'll learn about the Jewish marriage experience as it existed in Bible times. I believe it will inspire you. As we consider Jewish marriage customs, please keep in mind that customs are common practices observed by a defined group of people and are not necessarily followed in every situation.

The Bible alone is God's inspired and infallible Word (2 Tim. 3:16). As such, it stands in a category by itself and must remain the superior authority in all matters. Much of the historical background we'll consider comes from the Bible, but other historical information comes from reliable sources supported by biblical evidence. Unlike the Bible, these historical sources are fallible; they should never be given the same weight as God's Word, yet they do help us better understand Scripture.

THE JEWISH VIEW OF MARRIAGE

Before I began the in-depth historical research that led to this study, my understanding of ancient Jewish customs came from the wonderful musical, *Fiddler on the Roof.* "Fiddler" was the first live production I ever attended, and I can still remember my high school bus ride to it. In fact, I still occasionally get one of its catchy tunes stuck in my head.

Many years after that visit to the theatre, I began to explore the traditions the play's main character, Tevye, so passionately defended. God opened my eyes and revealed the divine significance of Jewish marriage customs by helping me understand the Jewish view of the marriage covenant and celebration.

In the next three paragraphs, underline key statements about the Jewish view of marriage.

From the beginning of their history, marriage has been an essential part of Jewish life. To Jews marriage is sacred, significant, and symbolic. Because they acknowledge that Elohim, God, designed marriage, this chosen people recognize it as a sacred priority. Moreover, they consider marriage "a holy covenant between man and woman—with God as the intermediary."[1] This sacred status of the marriage relationship forms the foundation on which most Jewish customs are based.

Marriage is significant not only as the foundation of families but because Jews believe it furthers the aim of growing in holiness—a goal so important that many Jews consider marriage an imperative or command.[2] Several cultural practices reflect this, including the fact that unmarried priests were not allowed to conduct Yom Kippur rights.[3]

Perhaps most importantly for our purposes, marriage in Jewish culture symbolizes God's relationship with Israel. We have already seen that God described His relationship with Israel in terms of a marriage relationship throughout the Old Testament, but we must understand that the Jewish people have long recognized God designed marriage, in part, to teach them spiritual truth.

THE JEWISH MARRIAGE EXPERIENCE

The spiritual truths reflected in the Jewish marriage experience apply to believers today just as those of times past. Let's start with the basics. During Bible times the Jewish marriage experience had three distinct phases. Each served a specific purpose and prepared the way for the next. Each phase reflects part of God's perfect plan to redeem His creation.

The Jewish marriage experience began with the *shiddukhin*–or arrangement–phase. *Shiddukhin* is an Aramaic term meaning "tranquility" and reportedly comes from the Jewish belief that a "woman finds tranquility in the house of her husband."[4] During this phase the potential bride was identified, the details of the arrangement were negotiated, and the betrothal covenant was ratified.[5]

Generally speaking, what part of the Bible describes the arrangement phase of Christ's relationship with the church?
○ Hebrews through Revelation
◉ Genesis through John
○ Psalms

At what point in the biblical narrative was the betrothal covenant between Christ and His church ratified, confirmed, or sealed?

New Testament – Christ's death + resurrection

The second phase is the *kiddushin*, which comes from a Hebrew root word meaning "sanctified or set apart."[6] This phase, also known as the betrothal, was a critical time of preparation for the marriage relationship as well as the upcoming wedding celebration. This period of physical and spiritual preparation began as the bride and bridegroom set themselves apart exclusively for one another. Although similar to a modern day engagement, the ancient Jewish betrothal was a more permanent arrangement that could be terminated only by death or divorce.[7]

Describe the first two phases in your own words.

shiddukhin: _bride selected   Arrangements made, betrothal covenant ratified_

kiddushin: _Bethrothal – permanent engagement   physical + spiritual preparation_

In the earlier activity Genesis through John corresponds with the arrangement phase. The betrothal covenant was ratified in the New Testament through Christ's death and resurrection, beginning the betrothal phase.

Nissuin is the third and final phase of the Jewish marriage process. Usually occurring about one year after the betrothal, this is the celebration phase. The word nissuin comes from the Hebrew verb *nasa*, which means "to be carried off, lifted up."[8] This final phase begins when the bridegroom returns to claim his beloved bride and includes the wedding celebration—one of the most joyous occasions in Jewish life.

I don't know about you, but these days my memory needs all the help it can get. The letters ABC help me recall the name of each of the phases of the Jewish marriage experience.

A for the Arrangement Phase
B for the Betrothal Phase
C for the Celebration Phase

Circle the phase that best describes the current relationship between Christ and His church.

If you answered "betrothal phase," you are absolutely right, but let me offer a word of caution. The Jewish marriage experience provides only a shadow of the spiritual truths represented—not a perfect reflection. In the words of the Apostle Paul, "Now we see but a poor reflection as in a mirror; then we shall see face to face. Now I know in part; then I shall know fully, even as I am fully known" (1 Cor. 13:12). One day we'll fully understand the marvelous mystery of Christ's relationship with His precious bride, the church. Until then, we have much to learn.

Day Three
The Wedding Party

During the remainder of this week, we'll explore the first part of the Jewish marriage experience: the arrangement phase. But first we'll meet the wedding party—those privileged to share in this exciting time of preparation and anticipation.

THE BRIDEGROOM

Biblical Background

In Old Testament times it was an honor to be the bridegroom; his role was central to the Jewish marriage process. As a key player, the groom enjoyed a special status which included, among other things, exemption from fasting on minor holidays.[9]

In spite of such luxuries, things weren't easy for a groom-to-be. Securing a suitable bride was rarely a simple matter; it required negotiations and planning. A son had to work closely with and under the supervision of his father to arrange a marriage. Judges 14:1-7,10-11 describe how one Old Testament figure worked with his father in planning his own matrimony.

What did Samson ask his father to do (v. 2)?

Saw a woman in Timnah, one of the daughters of the Phillistines & told his father to Get her for me as a wife

What custom did Samson fulfill when his father went to visit the woman (v. 10)?

Samson made a feast

Which of the following do you typically associate with feasting?
- ○ somber boredom
- ● joyous celebration
- ○ pouting displeasure

Search the Scripture

In Mark 2:18-20, what did the people ask Jesus?

Why do John's disciples & the disciples of the Pharisees fast, but your disciples do not fast?

Scripture doesn't say why others were abstaining from food, but Jesus made it clear fasting was not appropriate for the bridegroom's guests while He was with them. The bridegroom's presence and the joy of a coming union were reasons for celebration!

In describing Himself as the bridegroom, Jesus provided valuable insight into the uniqueness of His identity and the importance of His ministry. In claiming the special status of the bridegroom, Jesus set Himself apart from other teachers of the day. While John the Baptist had come to prepare the way, Jesus was the way (John 14:6). Although listeners may not have agreed about whether the disciples should fast, Jesus' immediate audience certainly understood His point: Rejoice, for the bridegroom is with you! I am He who was promised!

Surely chills ran down the spines of some in the crowd that day. Could this really be He? For if Jesus of Nazareth really was the bridegroom, His coming signaled the beginning of a special time on the kingdom calendar. Through Him a divine relationship would be established—a sacred relationship between God and humanity. Only through Christ could this new and everlasting covenant of love be sealed.

FRIEND OF THE BRIDEGROOM

Search the Scripture

Carefully read John 3:22-30. How did John the Baptist refer to Jesus in verse 29?

the bridegroom

Based on this passage, which of the following best describes John the Baptist's relationship to Jesus? *friend of the bridegroom*
○ an acquaintance ● a close friend ○ a brother

Here again we find the disciples of John the Baptist questioning Jesus' actions. Apparently concerned that Jesus' popularity would eclipse John's, they brought the matter to their leader's attention. I can't help but chuckle at the thought of John's disciples tattling on Jesus. Obviously, they didn't understand Jesus' identity, even though John plainly told them Jesus "is the Son of God" (John 1:34). Interestingly, they remembered that John testified about Jesus but apparently did not remember what he said.

John the Baptist knew Christ as few others did. In fact, he was the first to publicly proclaim Jesus as both the Son of God (John 1:34) and the Lamb of God (John 1:29). He was also the first to accept Jesus as the bridegroom. John enjoyed an intimate relationship with Jesus. He may have been the divine bridegroom's first true friend.

Discover the Meaning

Jesus wants each of us to know Him as our closest friend. In the Gospel of John, He elaborates on true friendship, providing a straightforward way to identify His friends.

Read John 15:9-17. In what ways does Jesus demonstrate His friendship with us (vv. 13,15-16)?

lay down his life for his friends; no longer made the Father known to us do I call you slaves, but I called you friends I chose you + appointed you to go + bear fruit (purpose)

How are we to demonstrate our friendship with Him?

Abide in Him + love one another

Did you notice Jesus *chose* us to be His friends? Even more exciting, He demonstrates His friendship toward us in three important ways: by giving His life, by making the Father known to us, and by appointing a purpose to our lives (John 15:13-16). Such a demonstration of friendship requires a response! A person cannot be a true friend of the bridegroom without first accepting Jesus as personal Savior and Lord.

THE BRIDE

Biblical Background

The bride also played a central role in the ancient Jewish marriage experience. Without her acceptance, the betrothal could not be finalized. Without her responsible attention, important preparations were left undone. Only the bride, having been chosen and prepared, could join her beloved in the wedding procession, taking center stage with him at the wedding feast.

Even in modern Christian weddings, much of our attention and resources are focused on the bride. When we hear about a wedding, our first thoughts usually concern the bride. Who is she? Is her bridal gown full-skirted or form-fitting? How will she look as she walks down the aisle? When my older daughter, Amber, married, it became apparent to me that many of the expectations and responsibilities for the wedding ceremony still revolve around the bride—and her mother.

Search the Scripture

Read Ephesians 5:22-32. To what is the relationship between husband and wife compared (v. 32)?

(husband)   (wife)
Christ and the Church

According to 2 Corinthians 11: 2, why was Paul jealous for the church at Corinth?

For I am jealous for you w/ a godly jealousy; for I betrothed you to one husband, so that to Christ I might present you as a pure virgin.

In comparing the relationship between Christ and the church to marriage, Paul identified the church—rather than the individual believer—as the bride of Christ. Paul also reminded the church she has been promised to one husband, Christ.

Some suggest the individual believer *is* the bride of Christ. I believe this interpretation is incomplete. The believer is an important part of the bride. Through personal friendship with the bridegroom, accomplished by personally accepting Jesus' free gift of salvation, an individual becomes a *part* of Christ's bride. According to Romans 12:5, "We who are many form one body, and each member belongs to all the others." What an excellent biblical definition of the church!

Discover the Meaning

I'm using the word *church* to refer to each local church as well as the collective church of which they are a part. Author Os Guinness explains: "It is not so much that there are different churches in different places as that there is one church in many places. Each local church embodies and represents the whole church, so the church is both local and universal, visible and invisible."[10]

You have already seen that Ephesians 5:32 speaks of the mystery of Christ and His church. In this passage, "mystery" means a divine truth that can only be revealed by God. According to Paul, God has partially revealed the profound mystery of the church through the marriage experience. Although we will not completely comprehend this mystery until Christ returns, the church's identity as the bride of Christ provides a valuable clue into God's overall plan.

THE ATTENDANTS

Biblical Background

Scripture first mentions bridal attendants in Genesis 24:61 when Rebekah's maids accompanied her to meet Isaac. Attendants served the bride by helping her prepare, watching for the return of the bridegroom, and sharing in the joy of the wedding feast.

Search the Scripture

In the parable of the wedding banquet (Matt. 22:13) and later in a parable concerning the last days (Matt. 25:1-13), Jesus referred to attendants.

> **Read Matthew 25:1-13. What is the main message of this parable?**
> ○ Wise attendants bring extra oil for those who don't have enough.
> ◉ Individuals are responsible for preparing for the bridegroom's return.
> ○ One cannot depend on others for help.

Without understanding the Jewish marriage process, we miss the meaning of the parable. Some have struggled with the idea that it portrays multiple brides. The parable of the 10 virgins actually describes 10 bridal attendants who waited for the bridegroom to return from his father's home to claim his bride. The parable describes believers as attendants to the bride of Christ, emphasizing the importance of individual responsibility in preparing for the bridegroom's return.

The responsibility to attend is not elective and cannot be delegated. Christ assigns us personal responsibility to help prepare the bride for His coming.

CHRIST ASSIGNS

US PERSONAL RESPONSIBILITY TO HELP PREPARE THE BRIDE FOR HIS COMING.

Make It Personal

The believer's multiple roles may seem confusing. How can one be a friend of the bridegroom, part of the bride, and attendant to the bride all at the same time?

Consider the multiple roles we play in our families. I serve as a wife, mother, daughter, sister, and grandmother. Even if you're not married or don't have children, you likely occupy multiple roles within your family too: daughter, sister, granddaughter, niece, or aunt. Sometimes these roles overlap, but they are easily distinguishable. Each role ultimately serves to strengthen the family unit.

Maintaining balance in our various family responsibilities can be difficult. The same is true of our different spiritual responsibilities. Some believers focus on their relationship with Christ and neglect their responsibilities to the community of believers; others pour themselves into the church, neglecting their personal relationships with Christ. Learning to value each responsibility helps achieve the balance God intended.

Rate each of your spiritual roles. Mark the spot on each line that most accurately reflects your life. Be honest. This is between you and God. You will not be asked to share this with your group.

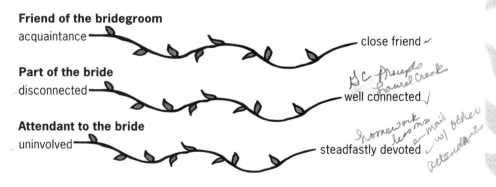

Friend of the bridegroom
acquaintance — close friend ✓

Part of the bride
disconnected — well connected ✓

Attendant to the bride
uninvolved — steadfastly devoted ✓

Based on your responses, what adjustments do you need to make to better fill your spiritual roles?

outreach

Don't get discouraged if you're not where you'd like to be. Filling our spiritual roles is a process, and we're each at different stages within that process. Praise God for helping you to identify your needs while leading you to learn more about Him.

Day Four
Terms of Relationship

Many of us love sentimental novels, so we sometimes think of marriage as the "happily ever after" to a storybook romance. But the ancient Jewish marriage experience began very differently than Western marriage relationships today. We need to put our romantic notions on hold.

Yes, love between the bridegroom and his precious bride would come. But in ancient times, wedding arrangements began with a father's love for his son.

THE OFFER OF RELATIONSHIP

Biblical Background

Read Genesis 24. According to verses 1-4, who initiated the marriage relationship between Isaac and his bride?

● Abraham   ○ Isaac   ○ Isaac's servant

Elderly Abraham initiated the process of finding his son a suitable wife. He took this responsibility seriously, choosing his most trusted servant to aid in the task and even requiring him to take a binding oath.

What most concerned Abraham about Isaac's future bride (vv. 3-4)?

that she not be a daughter of the Canaanites, but come from his country & his relatives

Make It Personal

Though the practice is still widely accepted in some parts of the world, the idea of a father choosing the bride for his son may seem foreign to us. To be honest, the thought of my husband, Roger, choosing a bride for our son, Taylor, makes me laugh. You see, I thought Roger would never get the nerve to ask me to marry him. It's even funnier to imagine him asking some fortunate young lady to marry our son.

During Bible times, however, the father or his representative chose the prospective bride, extended the offer of relationship, and negotiated the terms. This pattern resembles the way God the Father chose the bride for His Son. God initiates relationship with the bride but has no need to negotiate terms. The terms are clear and final: Will we accept His gift of salvation through Christ, or will we reject Him?

Beloved, that question still applies to each of us. We must each decide if we will agree to His terms or not.

Do I have an invitation to the wedding supper ceremony of Christ

yes

Have you personally responded to God's offer of relationship?

● yes   ○ no   If you answered no, please review page 154.

Review Genesis 24:8. The servant was released from his oath only if …

◉ the woman was unwilling
○ he got lost
○ war broke out

Describe the decision involved in Genesis 24:57-58.

her father + brother wanted Rebekah to wait 10 days before going w/ Issac's Servant, but they asked her what she wanted to do. She said she wanted to go now. She had the right to refuse altogether also.

I was surprised to learn that even though most Jewish marriages were arranged, a woman had the right to refuse the offer. In our example, Abraham's servant would actually be released from his oath if the woman refused. Fortunately for Isaac and for those of us who love happy endings, Rebekah accepted.

Discover the Meaning

According to *Essential Judaism*, the marriage contract "represents the agreement of a woman to give up a portion of her legal autonomy in return for a promise of financial support and other rights she receives from a man."[11] That partially explains why a prospective bride's consent was so important in early Jewish culture.

I believe the woman's right to refuse the offer of relationship illustrates several important spiritual lessons as well.

1. God extends the offer of relationship; we must choose whether to accept it.
2. We must each accept a personal relationship with Jesus Christ before we can become a part of His bride.
3. Should we accept that offer, we must give up our individual autonomy (self rule) to become part of the church.

Romans 12:3-5 describes this exchange of human independence for divine dependence. How would you explain these verses to a new Christian?

Believers are individuals, but one body in Christ

Eph 2:19 – members of God's household Christ Jesus is the Cornerstone

THE BRIDE PRICE

Biblical Background

Identifying the prospective bride was only the beginning of the Jewish marriage process, for gaining a wife proved an important and sometimes costly business transaction. The bride price, called *mohar*, was the price (in money or other valuables) that the father of the bridegroom or his representative was willing to pay to secure a bride.[12] The amount usually depended on several factors, including the bridegroom's family and social standing as well as the bride's desirability.

Search the Scripture

The Jewish custom of paying *mohar* is well documented in Scripture. Let's rejoin Abraham's servant in his search for a suitable bride for Isaac.

According to Genesis 24:10, what did Abraham's servant take with him?

10 Camels + a variety of good things of his master's hand

What was the bride price paid for Rebekah (v. 53)?

Articles of Silver + articles of gold + garments for Rebekah + precious things to her brother + mother

This was the first time we see *mohar* paid in the Old Testament, but it certainly won't be the last.

According to 1 Samuel 18:22-27, what unusual price did David agree to pay for King Saul's daughter, Michal?

100 foreskins of the Phillistines

What concern did David express about marrying the king's daughter?

I am a poor man + lightly esteemed from humble family lineage

Discover the Meaning

Although we cannot know for certain, society likely required a bride price for two important reasons. First, the price represented the bride's value to her family. After all, a capable young woman contributed significantly to her family in both economic and social terms. The bride price provided compensation to her family for this loss.[13] In other words, the price was truly a reflection of a woman's value. But *mohar* also served to secure the bride's future. It provided financial security for the bride should the bridegroom fail to complete the marriage covenant.

What did Christ pay for His bride according to 1 Peter 1:18-19?

the precious blood of Christ His Precious blood as of a lamb unblemished + spotless

Don't miss the important fact that the payment required for Christ's bride could not be satisfied by material things such as silver or gold. For His bride Christ paid the ultimate price: His own suffering, death, and resurrection.

You see, sin left humanity hopelessly separated from God. But God provided a way out of that hopelessness by allowing the penalty for our sin to be paid by another. Hebrews 9:22 reminds us that "without the shedding of blood there is no forgiveness" for sin. Christ's death was required to forever redeem His bride from sin's condemnation.

THE FAMILY PRESTIGE

When one of my children develops a romantic interest, the mother in me immediately wants all the details. One of my first questions is, "Does he or she come from a good family?" Such questions are met with deep sighs and rolling eyes, but during Bible times, Jews took this question very seriously.

Biblical Background

Scripture often introduces people in this manner: "Igal son of Joseph" (Num. 13:7). Jewish family prestige was generally acquired through distinguished ancestry; lineage was of great consequence. Partially for this reason, families kept detailed genealogical records.[14] The Book of Chronicles further demonstrates this record keeping, and Nehemiah 7 shows how meticulously family genealogies were reconstructed after the Jews returned from exile. Family ties helped define individuals.

With this in mind, it's not surprising that the issue of family genealogy played an important role in choosing a marriage partner.[15] For instance, Abraham was so concerned about family prestige that he insisted his servant find a suitable wife for Isaac among his own people. Given the opportunity to marry King Saul's daughter, David expressed concern about his lack of family prestige (1 Sam. 18:22-27). David understood it was no small matter for someone of his humble family lineage to become the king's son-in-law.

Discover the Meaning

Jesus the beloved bridegroom possesses a perfectly divine and royal family lineage: He is the Son of God and our High Priest (see Heb. 4:14). A Jewish bride—or any bride—couldn't ask for a bridegroom with a more impressive pedigree.

But what of humanity's prestige? What claim to greatness can the bride of Christ offer her bridegroom? My friend, without Christ, the church is simply a group of people who share a sinful family history of disgrace.

Only as a result of God's amazing grace extended to us through Jesus is our family prestige radically improved. Paul eloquently described this spiritual reality. In the Book of Ephesians he said, "Consequently, you are no longer foreigners and aliens, but fellow citizens with God's people and members of God's household, built on the foundation of the apostles and prophets, with Christ Jesus himself as the chief cornerstone" (Eph. 2:19).

WITHOUT CHRIST, THE CHURCH IS SIMPLY A GROUP OF PEOPLE WHO SHARE A SINFUL FAMILY HISTORY OF DISGRACE.

As you read each of the following Scriptures, circle the phrases that describe our family prestige through Christ:

"You are a chosen people, a royal priesthood, a holy nation, a people belonging to God, that you may declare the praises of him who called you out of darkness into his wonderful light" (1 Pet. 2:9).

"From Jesus Christ, who is the faithful witness, the firstborn from the dead, and the ruler of the kings of earth.

To him who loves us and has freed us from our sins by his blood, and has made us to be a kingdom and priests to serve his God and Father—to him be glory and power for ever and ever!" (Rev. 1:5-6).

Beloved, through Jesus' sacrifice, our family status is not simply enriched but miraculously transformed!

Make It Personal

Complete the following statements:
I would describe my earthly family lineage as …

_____

Based on who I am in Christ, my spiritual family lineage is … *royalty Children of the King*

A people belonging to God – a chosen people from Jesus Christ who loves me + frees me by His blood

Think about how the reality of this spiritual transformation affects your life. Mark the place on the line that best reflects how you live.

behave as a Representative of Christ the King

I live as one disgraced and without prestige. → I live as a member of a royal priesthood.

Unlike the Jewish marriage custom that based the price on a bride's desirability, God determined to pay the ultimate price for a bride with a lineage of complete disgrace. One believer at a time He transforms the church's family prestige, making her suitable to become Christ's bride. As you close your study time today, reflect on God's willingness to pay so great a price for the church—to pay such a price for you!

Record your thoughts.

Thankful + humbled + joyous + content grateful that He was willing to pay this great price for the church – for me.

Day Five
The Price He Paid

Imagine a young man's enthusiasm on taking his fiancée to meet his family. He met her at college and fell in love. Now they both beam with excitement as he offers his arm and leads her to the front porch. He says: "I can't wait for everyone to meet you! I just know that when they see how much I love you, they'll adore you too."

Christ deeply desires that we see how much He loves His bride so we can love her as He does. As we allow Him to tell us about His bride and His relationship with her, our thinking and actions toward her will change. We will learn to embrace the church—to cherish her—as He does. But we'll never understand the extent of Christ's love for His bride unless we first examine the price He willingly paid for her.

Allow Him to grow your love for the church by studying His love for her. Remember that you are not just a bridal attendant; you are also part of the bride.

Biblical Background

In ancient times, Jewish custom required at least partial payment of the *mohar* before the betrothal was considered binding. This payment was tangible proof of the bridegroom's honorable intentions. A promise of payment alone would not suffice.

THE PRICE OF SHAME

Search the Scripture

Scripture makes it clear that Christ willingly and fully paid the costly price necessary to secure the future of His beloved bride, the church. As we'll soon learn, that was no simple feat.

> **According to Hebrews 12:2, what did Jesus think of the shame attached to the crucifixion?**
> - ○ The shame didn't affect Him because He was God.
> - ○ The physical pain overshadowed the shame.
> - ● He scorned or despised the shame He had to go through.

Hebrews 12:2 does not suggest that the cross held no shame or that the shame had no affect on Christ. Rather, the shame of the cross was so intense that Jesus despised it. Being placed on a cross was incredibly shameful to the Son of God.

> **How do Deuteronomy 21:22-23 and Galatians 3:13 describe anyone hung on a tree?**

He who is hanged is accursed of God
Cursed is everyone who hangs from a tree

To redeem His bride, God's perfect Son endured the cruel humiliation of the cross. Pilate's soldiers, the chief priests, Herod and his soldiers, as well as those passing by that day taunted Him. Those to whom Jesus, Son of God and loving bridegroom, came to bring eternal life repeatedly mocked and scorned Him (see Mark 15:16-33; Luke 23:11). How painful it must have been to endure the insults of those He loved.

Carefully read Mark 15:16-32 and list three things Pilate's soldiers did to Jesus.

1. _dressed Him up in purple + put a crown of thorns on Him_
2. _beat His head w/a reed + spit on Him_
3. _crucified Him + divided up His garments among themselves_

Did Jesus have the power to come down from the cross? ● yes ○ no

Read Isaiah 53:7, which foretells Christ's sacrifice.
How did Jesus respond to the abuse?
○ angry protest ● silent acceptance ○ frustrated appeal

Jesus *willingly* submitted to relentless humiliation and shame to redeem His bride (see Matt. 26:47-56). At any time Jesus could have summoned help to stop the insults, could have retaliated for the cruel treatment, or could have left the cross. Amazingly, He chose to remain.

Make It Personal

Feelings of shame twist our stomachs in knots and make our cheeks burn. I still remember being ridiculed as a child because I had to wear thick eyeglasses. I was embarrassed by my poor eyesight and hated my glasses, but I desperately needed them. Some days I would stuff the glasses in my coat pocket before walking to school, pretending I could see without them and hoping to avoid teasing. Eventually, however, I was forced to put them on so I could read the chalkboard.

You may be experiencing shame and humiliation, or perhaps you can recall a time when you did. If so, briefly describe your feelings.

Board Minutes performancer review
wanted to be able to do better + meet
all expectations

Although painful, the worst humiliation you and I experience doesn't compare with what Christ suffered. Recalling our own humiliation, however, can bring greater understanding of what Christ willingly endured for His bride—what He willingly endured for you and me.

THE PRICE OF PAIN

Here I sit with my leg propped up. A few days ago I had surgery, and now I am experiencing a relentless, painful throb. My circumstances remind me of how weak our physical bodies can be and what little tolerance I have for even a little discomfort. I sit in amazement as I read Luke's account of the crucifixion, wondering how Jesus could so willingly endure unimaginable pain to pay His bride's price. How could He willingly pay so high a price for me?

Search the Scripture

Compare the events described in Luke 22:63-65 and John 19:1-3.

	Luke 22:63-65	John 19:1-3
Who was mistreating Jesus?	*the Men who were holding Jesus in custody*	*Pilate & the soldiers*
What did they do to Jesus?	*mocking Him & beating Him blindfolded Him blaspheming Him*	*Pilate scourged Him The soldiers put a crown of thrones on His head & a purple robe on Him, slap Him & mocked Him*

Just reading these passages makes me want to weep. Beloved, Jesus experienced a far greater degree of pain and suffering than I will ever know. Before being nailed to the cross, He was repeatedly and brutally beaten. The temple guards and Pilate's soldiers took turns viciously mistreating and mocking Him. At any point Jesus could have called it off. Instead, He willingly suffered unspeakable pain for His beloved bride. Why?

Because of love.

THE PRICE OF DEATH

Jesus understood the terms of *mohar* He must pay for His bride. He knew that the church could be redeemed only through a complete sacrifice. Jesus had to die, and He lived each day with full understanding of that reality. I've often wondered what that must have been like. Surely it was agonizing for Jesus to see sin in the world and to know it would cost Him His life.

Make It Personal

Read Mark 15:33-47. Why do you suppose Jesus cried out " 'My God, my God, why have you forsaken me?' "

He was in agony + felt alone

My soul grows quiet each time I ponder Jesus' death. The mixture of anger, sorrow, and guilt are almost unbearable. Adding to those feelings is the troubling question Jesus posed from the cross: " 'My God, my God, why have you forsaken me?' " Under what conditions would God forsake His beloved Son?

The answer underscores the seriousness of our sin. Jesus, who was God and was with God from the beginning, had never sinned (see John 1:1). In 2 Corinthians 5:21 Paul wrote, "God made him who had no sin to be sin for us, so that in him we might become the righteousness of God." Pause for a moment and try to envision what it was like for Jesus, who knew no sin, to become sin for us.

Describe what Jesus may have felt as He became sin for us.

_____

_____

"GOD MADE HIM WHO HAD NO SIN TO BE SIN *for us, so that in him we might become the righteousness of God."* 2 CORINTHIANS 5:21

As He died, Jesus bore the evil and wrongs of the entire world. I can't begin to imagine what that was like for Jesus–for God. Was Christ's bride worth such a price? His divine actions cried, "Yes!"

THE POWER OF RESURRECTION

When Jesus breathed His last, the final installment of the bride price was paid. Three days later, He demonstrated that the *mohar* was paid in full (Matt. 28:1-7). Can you imagine what indescribable joy the faithful women at the tomb must have felt upon hearing, " 'He has risen from the dead!' "? Friends, may we experience anew the sheer joy of the resurrection. The divine bridegroom has risen! He lives!

Make It Personal

Explain how knowing that Jesus suffered, died, and rose for you makes you feel.

Can never thank Him enough
Can never repay Him except do what He wants us to do - Attend the bride

Does the realization that Christ died because of His love for the church endear her to you? ⬤ yes ○ no Explain.

_____

Beloved, Christ demonstrated His love for the church by literally giving His life for her (Eph. 5:25). His sacrifice reflects the high value He places on her and reveals the depth of His love. We must understand that the church is priceless to Him.

As we close today's study time, consider this important question: What might Christ think about my attitude and actions toward His bride, the church?

Study Week
2
Meeting Week #3

2

Past Reflections of the Future

GROWING UP, I WAS ENTHRALLED BY MY MOTHER'S CEDAR-LINED HOPE CHEST. It held priceless treasures that provided exciting clues to my family heritage—personal items belonging to my great-grandparents as well as interesting mementos from my parents' school days and wonderful keepsakes from their wedding.

I often begged Mom to pull out the articles in the chest and to tell me all about each one. "Where did you get this old figurine?" I'd ask. "Why did you keep this red velvet baby dress? Where were you and Dad going the day this picture was taken?"

How I loved to hear her tell the story behind each precious keepsake! In some way, every item in that chest represented a part of me. Some of those treasures not only provided clues about my past but also hints about my future. My mother's delicate French lace wedding gown, for instance, would one day adorn an anxious young bride again on my own wedding day!

Much like my mother's hope chest, God's Word is full of treasures that explain our past and provide insight into our future. This week we will examine some of Scripture's precious contents as we seek to better understand God's plan for His church—His plan for you and me.

Day One
Symbols of Relationship

From the beginning God taught the Jews to be people of ceremony and celebration. Today many are still committed to His appointed observances. My former Jewish law partner, for instance, frequently attends annual religious gatherings. Some of these, such as *Yom Kippur*, are solemn. Others, like *Hanukkah*, are joyous. All acknowledge God and remind His people of their special relationship with Him.

The ancient Jewish betrothal ceremony was usually a formal and intimate gathering that publicly acknowledged the covenant relationship between the bridegroom and his bride. The ceremony marked the end of the *shiddukhin* and ushered in the *kiddushin*, or betrothal phase. I like to think of the ceremony in terms of a modern moment of engagement. But as we'll soon learn, this ceremony carried a weight and significance that today's modern betrothals seldom replicate.

THE MIKVEH

Biblical Background

Prior to their betrothal ceremony, the Jewish bride and groom separately prepared themselves to enter into covenant relationship. This preparation included the ritual of water immersion known as the *mikveh*.[1] Involving complete immersion into a river or a specially built pool, ritual immersion represented spiritual cleansing. This symbolic purification prior to entering into betrothal relationship underscores the important role betrothal played in Jewish life.

Search the Scripture

The Bible provides remarkable detail about Christ's betrothal of His bride, the church. Their sacred betrothal ceremony occurred during a very special gathering of Christ and His disciples. Only hours before He'd pay the mohar, Christ began their meeting with a beautiful act representing the pre-betrothal custom of the mikveh.

Read John 13:1-9. How do Jesus' words fit what you have learned about the betrothal process?

Spiritual Cleansing for the Covenant Relationship

I can't imagine a more appropriate preamble to the divine betrothal than John 13:1. A bridegroom would complete the betrothal and return to the father's house to await the time for the coming celebration. Jesus had long cherished His bride. Now the time to prove His enduring devotion and seal His promise approached. Don't miss the beauty of Jesus' actions. Humbly washing the feet of those who were hopelessly unworthy of Him, Jesus symbolically prepared the bride for covenant relationship.

For more information on ritual cleansing, see Leviticus 12–15, which describes many God-given regulations concerning ceremonial cleansing. These regulations resulted in a number of cleansing customs, including the separate cleansing of the bride and groom prior to the betrothal ceremony.

Discover the Meaning

The spiritual lessons reflected in the waters of the *mikveh* apply as well for us today. In preparation for her betrothal, Christ's bride, the church, must be spiritually cleansed. When Jesus washed the disciples' feet, He illustrated that only He Himself can provide thorough and everlasting cleansing.

Just as significantly, Jesus showed that we cannot be cleansed unless we allow Him to wash us. Perhaps you've heard the hymn, "Are You Washed in the Blood." The song refers to the powerful truth that when we accept Christ, we are cleansed of our sins by the blood Jesus shed when He died on the cross.

Believer's baptism reflects the same reality. Symbolic immersion in water occurs after one recognizes, confesses, and repents of sin and makes a conscious commitment of faith in Christ. This physical action represents the everlasting spiritual cleansing that results from accepting Christ as personal Savior and points to the fact that every believer actually becomes part of the bride. Much like the Jewish practice of ritual cleansing, Christian baptism represents spiritual cleansing.

THE SACRED CEREMONY

Biblical Background

While the details of the betrothal ceremony varied among families and geographic regions, the basic elements remained the same. The ceremony usually took place at the home of the bride's family[2] and normally included the bridegroom's presenting a gold ring or another valuable item to the bride (see Gen. 24:47).[3]

The betrothal ring symbolized a couple's mutual promise to remain exclusively set apart for one another. By placing a ring on the bride's finger [or in her nose] the bridegroom declared, "See by this ring you are set apart for me, according to the Law of Moses and of Israel."[4] In accepting the ring, the bride signaled her agreement to remain committed exclusively to her groom. The couple then concluded the ceremony with a shared cup of wine, symbolizing the blessing of their new covenant relationship.[5]

The ancient Jewish betrothal covenant was not a promise to marry; instead, it was the initiation of the marriage relationship. In this sense, the Jewish betrothal was much more binding than modern Western engagements. Continuing to live apart, the bride and bridegroom each prepared for the fulfillment of the marriage covenant. Once the betrothal covenant was established, however, the bride legally became the wife of the bridegroom. From that moment on, only the bridegroom had the option of nullifying the relationship.[6]

Search the Scripture

Scripture records Christ's prayer just prior to the blessing of His covenant relationship with His bride. As you read the following passage, keep in mind that *sanctify* means *to set apart* or *consecrate*.

Read John 17:13-19. For whom is Christ's bride set apart or sanctified?

○ for the angels   ● for Him   ○ for the world

On the very night that Jesus consecrated His bride, He blessed their relationship with a shared cup of wine. John does not record the details of the last supper. However, Matthew provides a helpful account of this special moment in the celebration.

Read Matthew 26:20,26-29. For you, how does understanding the betrothal covenant change the impact of these verses?

As the bride of Christ I am betrothed to Him

How did Jesus refer to this cup in Luke 22:20?

as the new covenant in My blood poured out for you

I hope you'll never see an illustration of the last supper again without recognizing that the event served as the divine betrothal ceremony! Don't miss the significance of this gathering. The disciples, the first members of the church, represented Christ's bride. Jesus, the bridegroom, lovingly presented the cup of His new covenant to them—a covenant that He would seal with His own blood. God the Father and all of heaven stood as holy witnesses to this historic event.

Jesus Christ offered a covenant like none the world had seen—an unending covenant that cannot be broken. In paying the bride price Jesus conquered death and opened the way to eternal relationship, promising never to forsake us (John 10:28; 14:18). That, my friend, is a powerful promise with an everlasting guarantee! (See Rom. 8:38-39.)

Discover the Meaning

Glance at Matthew 26:26-30. When did Jesus say He would again drink of the cup?
- ○ during the next Passover meal
- ○ after His resurrection
- ● when reunited with them in His Father's kingdom

Before the evening of celebration and promise ended, Jesus referred to the special cup He will share with His bride at their wedding celebration. This is significant to our study because during the Jewish wedding celebration that occurred sometime after the betrothal, the bridegroom shared a second cup of wine with his bride. Symbolizing the completion of the full marriage relationship, this was considered the cup of joy.[7] The joy of love. The joy of togetherness. The joy of a covenant kept.

I imagine a sense of sadness invaded the excitement as the Jewish betrothal ceremony drew to a close. As the bridegroom went back to his father's house to prepare a home for his bride, the young woman surely found her greatest comfort in his promise to return.

"DO NOT LET

YOUR HEARTS

BE TROUBLED.

Trust in God; trust also

in me. In my Father's house

are many rooms; if it were

not so, I would have told you.

I am going there to prepare

a place for you. And if I go

and prepare a place for you,

I WILL COME

BACK AND

TAKE YOU

TO BE WITH ME

that you also may

be where I am."

JOHN 14:1-3

When Christ went back to His Father's house, He understood the uncertainty the church would experience in His physical absence. The same night that Christ sanctified His bride and blessed the betrothal covenant, He offered the words of John 14:1-3 that appear in the margin. For the believer there is no greater promise.

If you belong to Christ, you will share the cup of divine joy with Jesus. One day we'll joyfully celebrate the bridegroom's return together! I can hardly wait!

Write John 14:1-3 on a note card. Carry it with you wherever you go, and let these words inspire and encourage you in the weeks ahead.

Make It Personal

You and I as believers must not forget that Christ set us apart from the world. He washed away our sin, called us His own, and promised to return for us. Together we compose His bride; our lives belong to Him.

Jesus Christ is preparing a place for us, and we must be prepared to meet Him. As we anticipate His return, we are responsible for avoiding things and places that could take our focus off Him. But even our best efforts to live sanctified lives—pure and holy lives—are useless without God's help. We must continuously ask Him to cleanse us and prepare us for the glorious wedding celebration.

What areas of your personal life indicate you are set apart for Christ?

daily devotions, bible study + meditation
, prayer   exercise + eat nutritious food in.
Thankfulness, love + devotion - healthy quantities of sins
faithfulness - Confession of sins

Circle the parts of your life you are holding back from the spiritual cleansing Christ offers.

family	work	habits	past hurts
emotions	talents	desire to succeed	lifestyle
thought life	ego	bitterness	relationships

How might refusing to let Christ cleanse those areas affect your commitment to the church?

I would not grow in holiness
He would not live in my heart

I pray you will accept the total cleansing Christ offers! Let Him wash away the sins, the hurts, and the struggles that keep you from rejoicing in the fact that you are His beloved. He will return for you!

Day Two

Record of Relationship

Before we begin today's topic, let's review what we've learned about the arrangement phase and betrothal ceremony.

Match the spiritual reality of Christ's relationship to the church with the basic elements of the arrangement phase.

Spiritual Reality of Christ's Relationship with Church

_d_ God chose Christ's bride.

_c_ Christ paid the bride price.

_a_ Christ and His church make a covenant.

_b_ The new covenant was sealed.

Jewish Marriage Experience

(a) Bride and groom agree to *(3)* remain set apart for one another

(b) Betrothal covenant sealed *(4)*

(c) Mohar paid *(2)*

(d) Father offers relationship *(1)*

Write the spiritual realities on the kingdom calendar illustration.

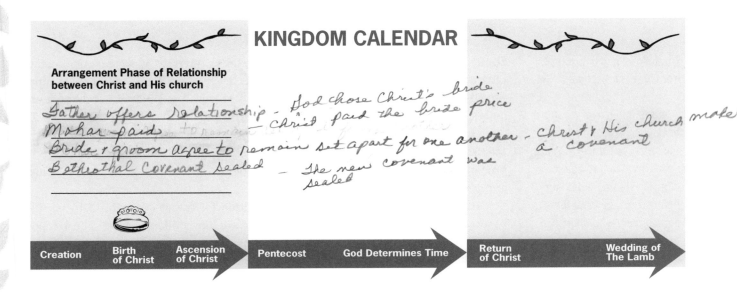

KINGDOM CALENDAR

Arrangement Phase of Relationship between Christ and His church

Father offers relationship — God chose Christ's bride.

Mohar paid — Christ paid the bride price

Bride + groom agree to remain set apart for one another — Christ & His church make a covenant

Bethrothal Covenant sealed — The new covenant was sealed

Creation | Birth of Christ | Ascension of Christ | Pentecost | God Determines Time | Return of Christ | Wedding of The Lamb

Yesterday we watched the betrothal ceremony draw to a close, leaving us with a strange mixture of anticipation and uncertainty. Surely the new bride experienced similar feelings as her beloved began the journey back to his father's house. Would she be ready when he returned? How would she remember his words and the promises they made?

The answers lay in another extraordinary blessing designed entirely for her protection. Let's explore this remarkable aspect of the Jewish marriage experience as our look at the *kiddushin*, the betrothal phase, continues.

THE *KETUBAH*

Search the Scripture

Read Malachi 2:13-15 in which God chastises a group of wayward priests. How does verse 14 refer to the marriage relationship?

○ arrangement　　◉ covenant　　○ burden

According to verse 15, what is God's role in the marriage relationship?

He made them one

God, as one who oversees a betrothal, unites Christ with the church, guaranteeing the completion of their sacred covenant relationship. Like a dutiful father, God acts as a witness requiring the faithful accomplishment of that agreement. Both roles highlight the importance God places on the marriage covenant.

Read Ezekiel 16:8. What kind of covenant did God make?

○ land purchase　　◉ betrothal　　○ peace treaty

Biblical Background

The following is an excerpt from an actual *ketubah*:

" I, Israel, the groom … affirm to be married to this Atika, the virgin, the bride … And I shall nourish, provide for, clothe, esteem. and honor her, in the manner of the Jewish men, who nourish, provide for, clothe, esteem, and honor their wives faithfully. She accepted and took upon herself … to serve, attend, esteem and honor him … in purity."

Some scholars believe *covenant* in these passages refers to a written document. Others feel the custom of writing the covenant began later. We do not know exactly when the Jews began putting marriage covenants in writing. We do know the written marriage covenant became known as a *ketubah*, which literally means "the writing."[8]

The *ketubah* is a formal document containing the terms of the Jewish marriage covenant.[9] Archeologists have discovered a marriage *ketubah* dating back to the time of Christ.[10] It details the responsibilities of the bridegroom as well as the bride and proves the marriage is legal.

Most scholars agree the *ketubah* was written for the sole benefit of the bride because it granted her important rights she did not have under the law.[11] The *ketubah* provided credible proof of the bride's relationship with the bridegroom. Without it, her future under the law was dangerously uncertain; she had no legal protection should her intended decide to back out of the verbal agreement. The promises made in her *ketubah*, however, were legally enforceable, giving the bride much needed peace of mind during the betrothal period and later during the marriage.

Please don't miss the significance of this point. The *ketubah* was priceless to the bride, guaranteeing her future, guiding her actions, and giving her hope.

Imagine you are a betrothed Jewish bride of ancient times. Describe your feelings regarding your precious *ketubah*.

peace of mind　　guarantees her future
legally enforceable　　life - changing document
hope
our peace + our certainty

God's word is our ketubah written for the benefit of the bride (the Church/the believer)

written document

The groom gave the *ketubah* to the bride immediately following the betrothal ceremony.[12] The only copy of her life-changing covenant with the groom remained with her throughout the betrothal period. Imagine how tightly she must have grasped the precious parchment as she watched her groom depart for his father's house. If she knew how to read, she surely read it repeatedly throughout the betrothal, treasuring every word. How encouraged she must have been by the precious promises of her beloved. *You are my bride. My wife. I will return for you.*

OUR SACRED WRITTEN COVENANT

Search the Scripture

After Christ returned to heaven, His disciples tried to remember everything He told them. Luke 1:1 tells us that many attempted to write about the events of Jesus' ministry. Some of these men, under divine inspiration, compiled important spiritual truth the church would need during the betrothal phase of the kingdom calendar. The good news they shared continues to teach and strengthen believers today.

> **Match the following things God's word does to the appropriate verses.**
> *B* abides in us bringing power   (a) Deuteronomy 10:13
> *C* teaches, encourages, and gives hope   (b) John 15:7
> *A* is given for our good   (c) Romans 15:4

The word *testament*, applied to the Jewish Scriptures (Gen. through Mal.) and the Christian Scriptures (Matt. through Rev.), comes from a Latin word meaning "covenant."[13] The Bible is literally the book of covenant and serves as the written expression of the sacred marriage agreement (*ketubah*) between Christ and the church. It contains all we need to know about Christ's relationship with His bride—the Father's pursuit of relationship, the Son's payment of *mohar*, the betrothal responsibilities, and the promise of everlasting joy upon the bridegroom's return.

God the Father carefully drafted and graciously delivered the sacred ketubah, the Bible, to the bride (2 Pet. 1:20-21). The church's precious *ketubah* guarantees her future, guides her present mission, and gives her hope for her bridegroom's return. Beloved, we can hold in our hands this priceless treasure!

Discover the Meaning

> **Read 2 Peter 1. Which of the following best explains why Peter wrote this letter about the truth of Scripture?**
> ● He wanted to remind believers of Christ's precious promises.
> ○ He needed reassurance that Scripture is true.
>
> **According to verses 20–21, what is the origin of all Scripture?**
> God through the Holy Spirit moved men to prophecy of Scripture

God's Word fills a vital role during this time of physical separation from Christ; it reminds us of His promises. Only God's Word offers us reassurance that we are loved by the God of the universe, that His Son paid the price of our sins with His own death and resurrection, and that Christ will one day take us to the wonderful new home He and His Father have prepared. As Christ's betrothed, we are to look to Scripture daily as our shining light in the world's darkness until He, the Morning Star, rises (Rev. 22:16). Until Jesus returns, we must remember that the Bible is a lamp illuminating the path of life, showing us how to live and reminding us of our purpose (Ps. 119:105).

> **Psalm 43:3 provides a wonderful picture of the work Scripture accomplishes during this time of separation. How does God's "light and truth" continue to guide the church today? (Mark all that apply.)**
>
> ● It leads us to Him.   ○ It keeps us entertained.
> ● It keeps us heaven-focused.   ● It supplies power for living.

Just as the promises in the *ketubah* guided the Jewish bride during the darkness of her betrothal separation, the Bible guides the church. Scripture is a light leading her to the holy mountain and the joyous wedding celebration, illuminating the path toward divine reunion with the heavenly bridegroom.

Make It Personal

> **According to Romans 15:4, what does Scripture give us?**
>
> *Hope*
>
> **Have you found hope in the Scriptures?** ● yes ○ no   If so, be ready to share an example with your group.
>
> **How does your church demonstrate the value of God's Word?**

[handwritten annotations: DC Precepts mann / Laurel Creek / telling others about Jesus / continually Be holy and Focus on Jesus — / By Studying God's Word to learn God's truth and / Participate in purposeful preparation   led by the Spirit]

Christ has entrusted His bride with a divine document—a gift more sacred and special than the world's most valuable treasures. God's Word cleanses, teaches, reminds, encourages, and gives hope.

Paul warned that a time would come when people would abandon Scripture for new teachers, new philosophies, new promises: lies that would forever dull them to the reality of Christ's love and soon return (2 Tim. 4:2-4). Unfortunately, we see that happening today. Some churches allow so much of the world into their hearts that they have left little room or desire for God's Word. They increasingly prefer man's wisdom to God's truth.

Beloved, the Bible contains all we need to know to successfully prepare for the bridegroom's return. Without it, we have no hope. I pray God will give us a fresh appreciation for His powerful, life-changing Word. May we never take our precious *ketubah* for granted!

Day Three
Purposeful Preparation

Today the church is in the second phase of the Jewish marriage experience, the *kiddushin*. As we seek to better understand God's plan for the bride of Christ and her attendants, we must comprehend the vital purpose betrothal served in Jewish life. That knowledge will open our minds to receive a greater awareness of the critical importance of our actions in this time of purposeful preparation.

THE GOAL OF HOLINESS

Search the Scripture

God's Word well documents Jewish betrothal tradition (Judg. 14:2-8; Matt. 1:18-21; 2 Cor. 11:2). Perhaps the most well-known example involves Mary and Joseph's betrothal. Their relationship provides valuable insight into marriage covenant customs practiced during the time of Christ.

Carefully read Matthew 1:18-25 and then review the following list of betrothal "facts." Put a star beside those the passage proves correct.

- ★ The custom of betrothal was practiced during the time of Christ.
    Only priests could perform betrothal ceremonies.
- Betrothed couples were not to have sexual relations.
    Betrothed couples wore special garments during the betrothal.
- ★ A divorce was required to end the betrothal relationship.
- ★ Remaining pure during the betrothal was a serious matter.

These verses reveal several points that help us better understand this unique time in the lives of a Jewish couple. First, notice that if Joseph chose to end his relationship with Mary, he was required to divorce her (Matt. 1:19). This confirms the binding nature of the betrothal relationship. Due to the unusual circumstances, Joseph took Mary home as his "wife," but the marriage was not consummated until after Jesus' birth (Matt. 1:25). This provides a clue into purity's significance during the betrothal. It also explains Luke's description of Mary and Joseph as "pledged" at the time of Jesus' arrival (Luke 2:5).

The Jews regarded the betrothal period as an exceptional time warranting special consideration. In week 1 we discussed special privileges given the bridegroom during his betrothal, such as exemption from fasting. But as we'll soon discover, betrothal also came with its own set of regulations.

Summarize the betrothal law presented in each passage.

Deuteronomy 20:7 *He must not go to war until married because if he died in battle, another man would marry her.*

Deuteronomy 22:23-24 _____

Deuteronomy 22:28-29 _____

This serious treatment indicates the vital importance of this preparation time. Notice that any man caught having sexual relations with a betrothed woman was put to death. However, had the woman not been betrothed, the man was only required to pay 50 shekels to the woman's father and marry her. This difference in treatment reflects the high priority Jews placed on purity during the betrothal period.

Discover the Meaning

While researching *kiddushin*, I discovered the key to the single-minded pursuit of purity that marked the betrothal: holiness. To be holy—perfect and spiritually pure—is the ultimate purpose of life for the Jew. In their book, *Under the Wedding Canopy: Love and Marriage in Judaism*, David and Esther Gross explain: "One of the great differences between Judaism and other religious faiths is the Jewish goal—in an individual, in a family, even in a whole community—of striving for holiness. The Bible teaches that God is holy, and also declares that God has made people in His image, and therefore all people must strive for holiness. This concept refers not only to prayer and formal worship but also directs the individual's attention to virtually every aspect of his/her daily life."[14]

Consequently, the ultimate goal of Jewish marriage is holiness. By following God's command to live together according to His standards for holy living and to rear children to live holy lives, the individual Jew moves closer to God.[15] This understanding underscores the importance of the betrothal phase. Remaining pure during the betrothal was absolutely essential to achieving holiness in marriage.

Recall that the Hebrew word for betrothal, *kiddushin*, means *sanctified* or *set apart, holy*.[16] Just as the Jewish bride was set apart to remain pure and singularly devoted to her bridegroom, Christ's bride, the church, should remain holy and focused on Him. She must remain pure, not allowing her commitment to Christ to be tarnished by growing more interested in the world than she is in Him. Her focus must be singular, not divided between affection for the bridegroom and a love for wealth and worldly pleasures (see Luke 16:13). *You cannot serve God and wealth*

Living pure lives is vitally important for believers. Preparation is the undisputed purpose of our current physical separation from Christ—our betrothal phase. The ultimate goal of our preparation is to grow in divine grace (holiness) as we get ready for His return. Scripture clearly teaches that "without holiness no one will see the Lord" (Heb. 12:14). I can't overemphasize the importance of steering clear of worldly things and philosophies that would turn our thoughts away from Christ.

Read 2 Corinthians 11:1-4. Describe the unfaithful behavior that caused Paul to reprimand the Corinthians (v. 4).

false preaching _____

_____

THE ULTIMATE GOAL OF OUR PREPARATION IS **TO GROW IN DIVINE GRACE (HOLINESS)** AS WE GET READY FOR HIS RETURN.

Glance again at the parable of the 10 virgins (Matt. 25:1-13). Explain what happened to those who did not prepare with committed focus.

The 5 who ran out of oil ~~they~~ *were late to the celebration and because they were not prepared they missed the celebration altogether.*

because they had to go + buy more oil for their lamps

Make It Personal

How would you characterize your church's emphasis on growing in holiness—remaining pure and set apart for Christ?

totally focused
love + commitment

How is remaining pure for Christ different than human efforts to be good enough to earn our salvation?

Purity is God's will for my life, not the way to salvation.

Which statement best describes your personal view of purity?
- ○ Purity is an old fashioned idea.
- ○ Purity is a good idea but not that important to me.
- ● Purity is God's will for my life.

TIME TO PREPARE

Biblical Background

Remaining set apart and pure during the time of betrothal was important for two reasons. First, it set up a standard of fidelity and faithfulness that would strengthen and bless the marriage as well as the couple's relationship with God. Second, it helped to cut down on distractions that might threaten the marriage preparation.

With much to be done and no time to waste, the betrothal period was filled with excited urgency. The bride and bridegroom each attended to important practical preparations during the betrothal phase.[17] He had an addition to build onto his father's house,[18] and she had wedding garments to prepare. But the most important part of the preparation was spiritual, as each spent time in introspection and contemplation.[19]

The bride and bridegroom took these preparations very seriously. Everyone understood that the much-anticipated wedding celebration would not occur until all preparations were complete.

Search the Scripture

According to Acts 1:7-8, what is the church's primary responsibility in preparing for Christ's return?
○ building bigger buildings
○ raising money for the needy
● telling others about Jesus

Before departing earth, Christ entrusted His beloved bride with a vital mission. The completion of that calling is a critical part of the bride's preparation. Christ's call to readiness is clear: His followers are to tell the world about Him as they excitedly await His return. This command to prepare is both individual and collective. The two are, in fact, inseparable.

Make It Personal

Explain how the call to tell about Christ was fulfilled through your life. Who led you to Christ? How? Plan to share your answer with the group.

Disabled Avon customers - a couple - both in wheelchairs + bibles in their laps

Love Worth Finding Ministry

Beloved, we are called to passionately labor to prepare the church. Like Paul and the early Christians, we must devote ourselves to sharing the message of eternal life with all who will listen: teaching, exhorting, and encouraging others to join us in preparing for Christ's return.

As we close today's study time, ask Jesus to continually remind you that you are set apart for Him. Tell Him how important His covenant promises are to you. Ask Him to give you the courage to tell others who He is and what He has done for you.

altar call at a Nazarene church as a teenager on a date

Day Four
The Father and Son at Work

Having played the busy mother-of-the-bride role, I have a fair understanding of the hard work and planning involved in getting the bride ready for her big day. But since I'll never be the father of the groom, I'm left to imagine what preparations that role might require. I can just picture Roger giving our son, Taylor, a heart-to-heart talk before such an event. They would likely sit down together, discussing everything from finances to the importance of daily telling his new wife, "I love you." Today we'll look heavenward as we consider the divine preparations of God the Father and Christ the bridegroom.

Biblical Background

Throughout the betrothal phase the bridegroom's father continued to play a central role in the Jewish marriage experience. He either prepared or assisted the bridegroom in preparing for the wedding banquet—a celebration that lasted up to a week and required careful planning (Judg. 14:10-11; compare Matt. 22:1-14). Interestingly, the bridegroom's father also determined the starting date for the wedding celebration (Matt. 22:1-14).

In preparing for the wedding of the Lamb, His Son's marriage banquet, God continues to play the central role. Like a bridegroom of ancient times, Jesus works closely with His Father (John 14:10): He does nothing on His own (John 5:19). Together, Father and Son lovingly prepare for the coming celebration.

DIVINE PREPARATIONS

Search the Scripture

Read 1 Corinthians 2:9-11. Why do you think the Lord is preparing such a wonderfully unimaginable place for the bride?
○ He enjoys following Jewish betrothal customs.
○ He is bored and has little else to do.
● He cherishes us and wants to lavish us with His love.

Do you think it is absolutely necessary that He prepare this elaborate new home for the bride? ● yes ○ no ○ I'm not sure. **Explain.**

for the completion of His eternal plan

Many times during my childhood my mother asked, "Martha, is that absolutely necessary?" Usually the question followed minor offenses such as playing my music too loudly as I dressed for school. The implied answer to this rhetorical question was always "of course not."

We can be assured that God's divine preparations are "absolutely necessary" to the completion of His eternal plan. Jesus told us His Father is *always* at work (John 5:19; 14:10). Even today He works to prepare the next phase on His kingdom calendar. Our God does not get off track; He does not forget the plan; He does not waste time.

Read the following verses and then explain the divine preparation each reveals.

Matthew 25:34 *inherit the kingdom prepared for you from the foundation of the world*

Matthew 25:41 *the eternal fire has been prepared for the devil & his angels*

1 Corinthians 2:9 *everything not seen, not heard, or felt is God has prepared for those who love Him*

Since "the foundation of the world," God has been diligently preparing for our future! Beginning with salvation in Christ and continuing into the glorious heavenly kingdom to come, wonderful future blessings await those who love Him. But just as thoroughly as God plans blessings for His children, He allows eternal separation for those who refuse to accept Him. God prepares harsh judgments, including eternal fire for unbelievers and the Devil and his angels. All are necessary to completing God's eternal plan.

Sometimes, in spite of Scripture's encouragements, we start to think these divine preparations are taking an awfully long time to complete. After all, didn't He prepare His kingdom before the world began? Isn't the eternal fire prepared for the Devil already glowing hot? Haven't over two thousand years of preparation time been enough for Christ to prepare a place for us? Our anxious human minds grow weary of the wait.

Discover the Meaning

What does Matthew 24:36 say about the timing of Christ's return?

But of that day & hour no one knows, but the Father alone

Scripture is clear that even the angels don't know when the divine bridegroom will come again. No one knows the day or the hour when He will appear. So even though the church's wait for Christ's return is sometimes difficult, we must trust that God alone has the sovereign right to choose the time for Christ's return.

Perhaps, like me, you sometimes wonder why Jesus is taking so long. Maybe you've glanced up at the sky on a particularly rough day and whispered, "Lord, this would be a great day to come back for us!" Although we cannot know for certain why Jesus has not yet returned, I believe Peter provided some insight that may help us to understand—and perhaps even appreciate—the wait.

According to 2 Peter 3:8-9, what is causing Jesus to tarry?

He wants none to parish but for all to come to repentance.

What would you say to those who made the statements in 2 Peter 3:3-4?

The Lord is patient toward you giving you time to make yourselves ready for His coming.

God the Father, not wanting anyone to perish, is patient, but His divine patience is only one important factor in our bridegroom's return. I find it significant that Peter connects the timing of Christ's return to the vital mission He gave the church. Jesus patiently waits for His bride to make herself ready for His coming. She's being given time to complete her mission, to prepare for reunion with her groom.

Later we'll look closer at the profound implications of the connection between Christ's return and the church's dual responsibilities to tell the world about Him and prepare herself for His coming. But as we conclude today's lesson, let's stay focused on what the divine bridegroom is doing during the time of betrothal.

According to Hebrews 7:23-25, what is Jesus doing on our behalf?

◉ pleading our case   *making intercession for us*
○ building palaces for us
○ making life easy for us

Everything the bridegroom did during the ancient Jewish betrothal demonstrated faithfulness to his bride. Through intercession, Jesus proves His devotion to His bride too. He intercedes for those who come to God through belief in Him and provides continuing opportunity for salvation throughout the generations. The church is called to share God's salvation with the world. Jesus faithfully supports His beloved bride through His unceasing intercession for the lost.

Make It Personal

Many of us have friends and family who have never come to a saving knowledge of Jesus Christ. As you continue to pray for those who don't know Him, be assured Jesus also desires that your precious loved ones be saved. Dear friend, at this very moment Jesus Himself stands ready to intercede for all who turn to God (Heb. 7:25). Praise Him for His faithfulness!

Please don't mistake Jesus' delay in returning as lack of interest. He longs to be reunited with His bride, to drink the cup of joy, and to rejoice with us at the coming wedding celebration.

Carefully read John 17:20-24 in the margin, noting each statement that indicates Jesus' desire to be reunited with us.

Can you hear the love and devotion in Jesus' voice as He pleads with His Father? Even before leaving for His Father's house, Jesus was thinking about the time when His bride would join Him in their new home. And He still longs to be reunited with His beloved church, faithfully doing all He can to help her prepare while eagerly awaiting His Father's command to bring her home.

Let's take a moment to connect a few important concepts that will help us see the bigger picture.

- Jesus' apparent delay in returning to claim His bride is related to God's mercy in not wanting anyone to perish (2 Pet. 3:8-9).
- Jesus continually and actively intercedes on behalf of those who seek salvation (Heb. 7:23-25).
- Jesus desires to be reunited with His bride (John 17:24).

By connecting these spiritual truths, we discover a beautiful portrait of unfailing faithfulness. Jesus' intercession is a labor of true love; each new believer brings the divine bridegroom one step closer to blessed reunion with His bride. What a marvelous reunion that will be!

" 'My prayer is not for them alone. I pray also for those who will believe in me through their message, THAT ALL OF THEM MAY BE ONE, Father, just as you are in me and I am in you. May they also be in us so that THE WORLD MAY BELIEVE THAT YOU HAVE SENT ME. I have given them the glory that you gave me, that they may be one as we are one: I in them and you in me. May they be brought to complete unity to let the world know that you sent me and have loved them even as you have loved me. Father, I want those you have given me TO BE WITH ME WHERE I AM, and to see my glory, the glory you have given me because you loved me before the creation of the world.' "

JOHN 17:20-24

Day Five
The Transforming Work of the Spirit

Yesterday we explored the divine preparations of God the Father and Christ the bridegroom. Today we shift our attention to the third member of the Trinity: the Holy Spirit. A constant companion to the bride of Christ, the Holy Spirit resides in each believer. The Spirit's power and presence surround the bride, producing sweet fruit and identifying her faithful attendants (see Gal. 5:22-25).

One lesson cannot adequately cover the all-encompassing work of God's Holy Spirit, but today's study lays important groundwork for future digging. Let's begin by pressing the rewind button to take a closer look at one special detail of the ancient betrothal ceremony.

THE MARK OF THE COVENANT

Biblical Background

Covenants in Bible times were usually confirmed by an identifying sign or mark. For example, a rainbow identified God's covenant with Noah (Gen. 9:12-13). Circumcision marked God's covenant with Abraham (Gen. 17:9-13). In much the same way, the betrothal covenant was also marked by a sign or symbol.

Recall that during the betrothal ceremony the bridegroom gave his bride a gold ring that would remain in her possession throughout the betrothal.[20] That ring identified her as belonging exclusively to him and served as a sign of their holy covenant. While researching pictures of ancient betrothal rings, I've found that many were unique and distinctive in design. The betrothal ring's uniqueness beautifully illustrated the bride's agreement to remain separate, unique among all women.

Various rings used throughout the Bible marked identity, status, and authority. Often rings were uniquely designed for their owners, serving as a distinguishing mark or personal seal. King Xerxes used such a ring to mark his approval of important documents (Esth. 3:12). Pharaoh also had a signet ring that he placed on Joseph's finger as a sign of the special authority bestowed on him (Gen. 41:41-42).

To learn more about the use of ancient rings, look at the following Scriptures: Genesis 38:18, 25; Esther 8:8; Ezekiel 16:8-12.

Discover the Meaning

Read 2 Corinthians 1:21-22 and Ephesians 1:13. How, as followers of Christ, have we been marked as belonging to God?

God sealed us + gave us the Spirit in our hearts as a pledge

Paul described the Holy Spirit as God's seal of ownership. I believe that just as the ring marked the Jewish betrothal covenant, the Holy Spirit signifies the divine

❀ *Attending the Bride of Christ*

betrothal covenant. The Holy Spirit, actively working within the church, marks us as belonging to God.

In day 1 we discovered some of the elements of Christ's divine betrothal to His bride as recorded in the Gospels. Recall that these events occurred during a very special gathering of Christ and His disciples just hours before His crucifixion. I saved one interesting detail concerning this divine betrothal for today's lesson.

Read John 14:15-17,25-27. Based on what we've learned, why is it significant that Jesus promised the Holy Spirit during this gathering at the last supper?

The Helper Spirit will teach you all things, + bring to your remembrance all that I said to you.

If the Holy Spirit is the spiritual mark of the new covenant with Christ, what is an outward manifestation of our covenant relationship with Him? (Hint, check Gal. 5:22-26) *The fruits of the Spirit*

love, joy, peace, patience, kindness, goodness, faithfulness, gentleness, self-control

2 Peter 1-8

The fruit of the Spirit proves the Holy Spirit working in our lives. Jesus taught that we are recognized or identified by our fruit (Matt. 7:16; 12:33; compare Luke 6:43-45). Love, joy, peace, patience, kindness, goodness, faithfulness, gentleness, and self-control are the observable characteristics of Christ's bride. These qualities identify the church as belonging exclusively to Christ.

Fallen humanity naturally tries to bargain with God; we seek to prove our own worth. How does seeing the fruit of the Spirit as evidence of your betrothal rather than assistance for your attempts to be "good enough" change your attitude?

I am joyfully allowing the Holy Spirit to influence everything I think and do so I will be worthy to attend the celebration in the new Kingdom as the bride of Christ.

Make It Personal

Based on the fruit of the Spirit listed in Galatians 5:22-23, how clearly does your church identify herself as belonging exclusively to Christ?
- ○ My church rarely exhibits the fruit of the Spirit, providing little evidence we belong to Christ.
- ○ Sometimes my church evidences the fruit of the Spirit and sometimes it doesn't. As a result, it is often unclear whether or not we belong to Christ.
- ● My church frequently displays the fruit of the Spirit, evidencing that we belong to Christ.

How well are you, based on the fruit of the Spirit, identified as part of Christ's bride?

○ I'm obviously a devoted believer. *—hopefully*

◉ Some days I'm more easily identified as part of the bride than others. *realistically*

○ I'm not sure that anyone knows I'm a Christian.

◉ Other *pray everyday for a Spirit – filled personality*

The church's preparation involves a divine transformation accomplished both individually and collectively among the community of believers. The Holy Spirit plays a critical role in that preparation.

WORKING THROUGH US

Search the Scripture

The Bible explains that the Holy Spirit lives in each believer (Rom. 8:9), providing the power necessary to fully prepare for Christ's return. List characteristics of the Holy Spirit revealed in the following verses.

While Jesus is away from us, the Holy Spirit will be our Counselor

John 14:15-17,25-26 *love, Helper, truth, abides in me & I abide in Him, teacher*

John 16:5-15 *Helper, convicts the world of counselor intercedes for us. Sin, righteousness & judgment, Spirit of truth will guide us in all truth. Glorifies God. will disclose all He hears from God to us.*

If you desire to know more about the Holy Spirit, see these verses:

Romans 8:26-27 ✓

1 Corinthians 2:9-14 ✓

Ephesians 3:16-19 ✓

Although Jesus patiently explained to His disciples that the Holy Spirit would serve as Counselor during this time of physical separation, they were understandably confused. Jesus described something they had not yet personally experienced. *How,* they surely wondered, *could anything be better than Jesus' physical presence among us?* But what the disciples failed to comprehend was that Jesus was speaking of the Holy Spirit of God literally living within and actively working through them. The indwelling of the Holy Spirit was a radically new spiritual truth they would better understand after the Day of Pentecost (see Acts 2:1-4).

Discover the Meaning

Preparing for Christ's return requires the Holy Spirit's supernatural power. It simply cannot be done without Him! Living in us, the Spirit works to transform us from the inside out. Guiding the individual believer and the church in all truth, teaching all things, reminding us of the bridegroom's words, and telling what is yet to come, the Holy Spirit is a powerful helper. But the Spirit only works where we allow Him to. He does not impose Himself on anyone. Instead, He is a true gentleman patiently waiting for us to yield to Him.

God wants us to know more of His Holy Spirit, to cling to His help and to trust His guidance as we prepare for the bridegroom's return. Like the disciples, I have difficulty comprehending the Holy Spirit's awesome, supernatural work. But for some time now, God has led me to pray that He will teach me more about life in the Spirit. I have been overwhelmed by His response.

Match what each of the following Scriptures reveals about the Holy Spirit's work.

<u>c</u> Acts 9:31   (a) guides

<u>b</u> Acts 13:1-3   (b) appoints

<u>a</u> Acts 20:28-29   (c) encourages

Though He works within the lives of individual believers, the Holy Spirit is actively involved in the church. In New Testament times the Spirit not only appointed leaders but He also strengthened, encouraged, and spoke directly to the church. Additionally, He convicts the world of sin (John 16:8-11), assisting the church in completing her mission of spreading the gospel as she prepares for Christ's return. This same Spirit that arrived at Pentecost ministers in and through the church today. But will the bride allow the Holy Spirit to work?

Make It Personal

How would you explain the indwelling of the Holy Spirit to a new believer?

Your Helper is learning the truth and is preparing for Jesus' return

How can you tell when the Holy Spirit is at work in your life and church?

by their fruits

How would you rate your church's current openness to the Holy Spirit's work?

not very open ————————————————— actively seeking and following

I warned you we wouldn't be able to condense everything about the Holy Spirit into one lesson. But aren't you thankful He is too big for that? Let's give Him plenty of room to work in the weeks ahead as He demonstrates how essential He is in the life of the believer and the church. May we allow Him to influence everything we are and all we do.

Study week #3
pts #4   6/27/11
no mtg 7/4/11

3

The Divine Partnership

A FEW YEARS AGO I WENT HANG GLIDING OFF THE SWISS ALPS. I'll never forget the breath-taking exhilaration of being carried away by the wind as the exquisite landscape spread below. As I soared between the mountains, I felt as if I were floating on my own power, but I knew better. A specially trained hang glider pilot carefully kept us above the treetops. Checking our speed and monitoring the wind currents, he remained in full control. By following his instructions, I landed safely–breathless with excitement and awestruck by the beauty that surrounded us.

That hang gliding adventure reminds me of the value of partnership. When I relied on the expertise and experience of my hang gliding partner, I was able to do something I could never do on my own: I was able to "fly." Although I couldn't always see him, I knew my trainer was right beside me, shouting encouragement and delighting in my obvious joy.

You and I are in divine partnership with God, sharing in a relationship that enables us to do wonderful things we could never do without Him. With God's help, we can exchange years of meaningless mediocrity for purposeful lives filled with God-sized adventure! We can experience the joy of knowing He uses our lives to accomplish His eternal plan.

This week we'll seek to better understand divine partnership with God while considering our personal role in preparing for Christ's return.

Day One
Fellow Workers

We've seen that in ancient Jewish weddings, many people—including the bride and groom, the groom's father, and the bride's attendants—worked together in preparation for a coming marriage. Today we will use what we've studied to answer two important questions: What is required to prepare for the bridegroom's return? How are we to individually respond to Christ's call to readiness?

Biblical Background

While the bridegroom and his father prepared, the bride not only sewed beautiful wedding garments but was to consecrate herself in the true spirit of the betrothal time.[1] Keeping herself set apart—physically and spiritually pure—was her most important betrothal responsibility. She had made a solemn oath to her beloved: He counted on her to be ready when he returned.

The bride was not alone in her work. Jewish tradition required the entire community to be involved in bringing joy and happiness to the bride and bridegroom.[2] Attending the bride as she prepared for the holy covenant of marriage was an honor: it provided opportunity to further the community goal of holiness.

With this in mind, it's important to note that individuals within the Jewish community did not consider the task of attending the bride as drudgery. It was a joy to serve—a privilege to be part of the celebration.

THE CHURCH COMMUNITY

To appreciate God's preparation plan for Christ's bride and our role in it, we need God's understanding of church. Not simply an organization we join or a weekly service we endure, church is a part of who we are as believers in Christ. We need the church, and the church needs us (see 1 Cor. 12:12-26). God intends that every believer be a participating member of the church body. We are each responsible for attending to her needs.

The early believers devoted themselves to the church—a factor that proved essential to the early church's effectiveness (see margin). Early Christians faithfully attended the church, and you and I must do the same.

Discover the Meaning

Unfortunately, faithful participation in church life has become optional for many believers. The majority of us tend to serve the church at our personal convenience—doing only what we feel like doing, when or if we feel like it. Even those of us who desire to serve faithfully often face difficult choices. Our culture and lifestyles aggres-

The word "devoted" used in Acts 2:42 ("they devoted themselves to the apostles' teaching, to fellowship, to the breaking of bread, and to prayers") is from the Greek word *proskartereo*, which is also translated "attend" or "attended." *Proskartereo* means "to give unremitting care to [something]"[3] Another source defines the term as "To stick faithfully with someone ... used metaphorically of faithfulness in the disciplines of the Christian life."[4]

sively compete for our time and attention, resulting in a kind of selective service that can benefit the church body but falls short of the steadfast devotion God expects.

Note how Romans 16:1 describes Phoebe. What was a servant's role?

to serve the church

Several different Greek words are translated "servant." The word in Romans 16:1 is *diakonos*, which "emphasizes the individual attention given in the service of another, and it carries a note of affection or devotion."[5] Each believer is called to be a devoted "Phoebe," faithfully working toward the eternal joy and happiness of the divine bridegroom and His bride. That devotion is demonstrated through sacrificial service not limited to what takes place inside church buildings. Devoted service to Christ and His bride reaches into every aspect of our lives.

How would you describe the difference between selective and sacrificial service?

_____

_____

Mark the place on the line that best identifies how often you sacrificially serve your church.

never ——— seldom   regularly ——— often

We must realize that a believer's lack of active participation and enthusiastic service in the work of the local church has profound consequences for both the believer and the church body. The church is like a blazing fire ignited by the Holy Spirit and fueled by each believer's passion for Christ. Separated from other believers, Christians become spiritually cold and lifeless; the church is diminished by their absence (see 1 Cor. 12:14,26; Heb. 10:24-25). When believers return and contribute, they are rekindled, and the collective blaze burns more brightly.

Make It Personal

A wise young pastor explained the believer's call to community. He challenged listeners to do three things: connect, commit, and contribute. We as Christians must connect with a local church, going even when it's not convenient. We must commit to living for God and to fulfilling His purpose for our lives. And we must contribute to the church by finding and filling our places of service (see margin).

Think of attending Christ's bride as a group project with individual assignments. The final outcome depends on the full participation of all group members and their ability to work together. By God's design the actions of both the individual believer and the church are equally important. What we do—what you do—matters.

I COMMEND
TO YOU
our sister Phoebe,
who is a servant of the
church in Cenchreae.
ROMANS 16:1

Service is not a task but an extraordinary gift that brings a richness to our existence. Jesus told us that because we're His friends, He has appointed our lives with meaning and purpose (John 15:14-16). This purpose includes the indescribable privilege of working with God to accomplish His eternal plan. Beloved, if you spend your life serving Him, you will find your worth in Him.

THE DIVINE PARTNERSHIP

Search the Scripture

Our life-long purpose is to prepare Christ's bride, willingly serving as we make ready for His return. But we must never make the mistake of thinking that the church's preparation rests entirely on our shoulders. We don't work alone. You and I are part of a divine partnership with God.

Read 1 Corinthians 3:6-9 for insight into how this partnership works.

What did Paul try to teach the church at Corinth? (Check all that apply.)
- ○ Planting and watering are not important.
- ◉ Those who plant are important.
- ◉ God is the one who gives the growth.
- ◉ We are coworkers with God.

We already learned that we should work as servants within the church. First Corinthians 3:9, however, explains that we are "God's fellow workers." What do you think that means?

_____

See the verse in the margin. Who supplies the desire and the power for this divine partnership?
- ○ the pastor   ○ the individual believer   ◉ God

For whose purpose are we intended? _God's good purpose_

Understand that this divine partnership is not an equal partnership. Only God's participation is necessary (1 Cor. 3:7). We can do nothing for God that He cannot do for Himself (Acts 17:24-25). Let's pause and allow that to sink in. God doesn't need but rather *graciously* allows our participation for our benefit.

I'm reminded of when my children were young and wanted to "help" me in the kitchen. Not only did I not need their "help," but their involvement in my cooking made everything more challenging. I discovered, however, that allowing them to assist me brought the joys of shared experiences, treasured memories, and strengthened relationships. In much the same way, God allows us to work with Him in divine partnership, bringing us joy, reminding us of His faithfulness, and strengthening our relationship with Him.

Service is not a task. It's a privilege! Here are a few ways you can serve your church.
- Write notes of encouragement to visitors.
- Volunteer to help in the church office.
- Host a baby shower to meet the needs of the nursery.
- Participate in a work day.
- Help prepare meals for the sick and elderly.
- Join the choir or orchestra.

"FOR IT IS GOD

who is working in you,

|ENABLING YOU|

BOTH TO WILL

AND TO ACT

for His good purpose. "

PHILIPPIANS 2:13, HCSB

"**IF YOU LOVE ME,**

you will keep

My commandments

And I will ask the Father,

and He will give you another

Counselor to be with you

FOREVER. …

The one who has My

commands and keeps them

is the one who loves Me.

And the one who loves Me

will be loved by My Father.

I also will love him and will

reveal Myself to him. …"

"**IF ANYONE**

LOVES ME,

he will keep My word.

My Father will love him,

and We will come to him and

make Our home with him.

The one who doesn't love Me

will not keep My words.

The word that you hear

is not Mine but is from

the Father who sent Me.

JOHN 14:15-16, 21, 23-24,

HCSB

I wish it were possible to provide a simple rule to follow in expressing what God really wants from us in the divine partnership. But the call to readiness is intentionally based on relationship rather than rules or formulas. Our role in the relationship revolves around one action: obedience.

> **Read John 14:15-16,21,23-24. What can we learn from this passage?**
> ◉ Love results in obedience.
> ○ We should not obey men.
> ○ We should teach others to obey.

Jesus leaves no room for doubt: "If anyone loves me, he will obey my teaching" (John 14:23). Our obedience to His commands and our faithfulness to keep His Word demonstrate our love for Him. If we truly love Jesus, we will gladly and wholeheartedly tend His bride. At this point many of us may feel a little uneasy. Obedience is a difficult lesson to learn and a hard lesson to hear.

All of us, at one time or another, have rebelled against parents, rules, and God. Most of us have tried to reform. In fact, we do our very best to obediently follow the Lord. We read Scripture and truly try to be like Jesus, yet we fail.

> **How do efforts to reform in order to be good enough for God differ from efforts to honor God because He has already accepted us?**
>
> _____
>
> _____

God has news we all need. Even with the best of intentions and effort, we're not capable of the pure obedience He requires. Real obedience comes from love. It does not make us acceptable to God. He has accepted us purely by His grace. We are not, however, excused from trying our best.

> **Read Romans 7:14-20. Which of the following best summarizes Paul's struggle with obedience?**
> ○ He sinned because he enjoyed sinning.
> ◉ He sinned though he knew better and didn't want to sin.
> ○ He sinned because the Devil made him do it.

Paul's words cause me to wonder how I could ever fill my part in the divine partnership. How often I mess up and find myself angry and frustrated over my shortcomings!

> **What encouraging insight does John 15:5 provide about our role in the divine partnership?**

Apart from Jesus, we can do nothing
He is the Vine; we are the branches
Abide in Him

Friends, apart from God we have nothing to offer Him. Yes, we're called to obedience, but we are not capable of complete obedience in our own strength. Only in the power of God's Holy Spirit can we fully obey. Remember that in John 14:15-16 Jesus' command to obey included the promise of the Holy Spirit. God understood we would need His help to be obedient, and He sent the Spirit to meet that need.

Read Romans 8:5-13. According to verses 12-13, what is our obligation to the flesh as followers of Christ?

the mind set on the flesh is death
the mind set on the Spirit is life + peace
Put to death the deeds of the body and you will live

allow the Holy Spirit to control my life

When we allow the Holy Spirit to control our lives, we fulfill our obligation to the divine partnership. By helping us obey, He empowers us put our love for Christ in action. He inspires us to serve Christ and His bride with joy and gladness.

Make It Personal

Perhaps a personal illustration will best conclude our look at divine partnership. When my son, Taylor, was about four, he loved to "help" his dad mow. You can imagine his excitement when Roger began to allow him to ride along on the mower. Each time Taylor proudly announced to the household, "I need to help Dad." Of course Roger did not *need* Taylor's help. But because he loved his son, he allowed him to ride along, sometimes even letting Taylor think he was operating the controls. (Of course, Roger was always in charge.)

On his own, Taylor had nothing to offer his father except obedient surrender to Roger's control of the lawn mower. And even though Taylor did not realize it, that simple yet important act of obedience was an extension of his father's loving influence over him. This precious partnership between father and son grew into a loving relationship that helped our family through the tough teen years.

Think about your experiences with God. Describe an example of divine partnership at work in your life.

_____

_____

_____

While preparing this lesson, I gained a much better understanding of why God alone is essential to the success of the divine partnership. He is the Heavenly Father. And just as Taylor was dependent upon his earthly parent's control, I am thoroughly dependent on my Heavenly Father's control. I'm very thankful God's plans are not dependent on me, and I'm equally thankful He graciously allows me to participate with Him.

Let's commit to trusting God in obedience this week as we further explore Christ's call to readiness.

Day Two
Measuring True Readiness

Before we begin our look at true readiness, let's update our kingdom calendar.

Match the spiritual reality of Christ's relationship with the church and the corresponding elements of the betrothal phase.

Christs's Relationship with His Church

d The church is called to prepare for Christ's return.

A Christ works with His Father to prepare.

B The church is spiritually prepared as believers join together with God.

C Individual believers attend the bride of Christ through the Holy Spirit's power.

Jewish Marriage Experience

(a) The bridegroom works with ② his father to prepare.

(b) A time of important spiritual ③ preparation takes place.

(c) Family and friends attend ④ the bride.

(d) The bride prepares her ① wedding garments.

Place the spiritual realities of the betrothal phase on the kingdom calendar.

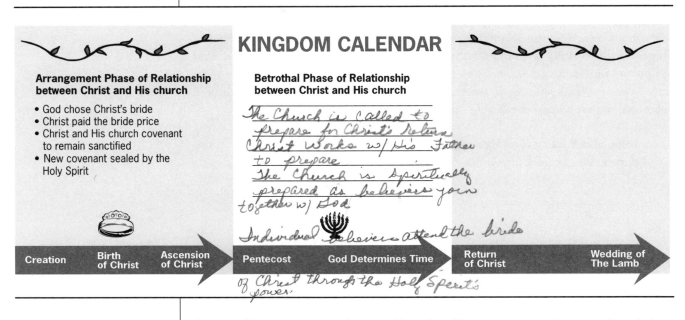

KINGDOM CALENDAR

Arrangement Phase of Relationship between Christ and His church

- God chose Christ's bride
- Christ paid the bride price
- Christ and His church covenant to remain sanctified
- New covenant sealed by the Holy Spirit

Betrothal Phase of Relationship between Christ and His church

The Church is called to prepare for Christ's return
Christ works w/ His Father to prepare
The Church is Spiritually prepared as believers join together w/ God
Individual believers attend the bride of Christ through the Holy Spirit's power

| Creation | Birth of Christ | Ascension of Christ | Pentecost | God Determines Time | Return of Christ | Wedding of The Lamb |

One challenge to responding to Christ's call to prepare is that we often fail to accurately measure our state of readiness. We can sincerely believe we're ready to meet the bridegroom yet remain woefully unprepared for the encounter. The obvious danger in failing to gauge our preparedness is that we might cease to prepare, becoming like the unwise virgins who took no oil for their lamps (see Matt. 25:1-13). Today we'll consider elements of true readiness that will help us more accurately measure the quality of our preparations.

THE PURPOSE OF HUMILITY

Search the Scripture

Read Luke 22:31-34,54-62. How did Peter respond to Jesus' statement, " 'Satan has asked to sift you as wheat' " (v. 33)?

Lord, with you I am ready to both go to prison & to death.

What happened when that sifting time came?
- ○ Peter demonstrated his faithfulness to Christ.
- ● Three times Peter denied even knowing Jesus.
- ○ Because Jesus prayed, Peter was able to avoid Satan's testing.

We can learn valuable readiness lessons from Simon Peter. Jesus warned that Satan was planning to try him. With great confidence (and little thought) Peter replied, "Lord, I'm ready to go with you to prison and to death."

Jesus knew Peter was not ready, and his illusion of readiness stood in the way of much-needed preparation. When Peter's readiness was put to the test later that night, he lacked the strength to stand with Christ. Peter, who thought he was ready to die with Christ, would not even admit to knowing Him.

I believe this passage shows how God was working to prepare Peter for what was to come. Notice Jesus' prayer for Peter (v. 32); He did not ask that Peter be saved from the testing, but that Peter's faith would not fail. This testing had a divine purpose. Although Peter probably thought he failed Christ in this situation, I believe Jesus saw his humbling ordeal as part of the refining process. When Peter thought things were falling apart, Jesus knew they were just falling into place.

Proud, boastful Peter was not ready to obediently serve in the church after Christ's resurrection. By his words we see that Peter held to a false sense of readiness that would have proved a tremendous obstacle in the challenging days and years ahead. But recognizing his own weakness through the fulfillment of Jesus' words humbled Peter. As a result, he became more aware of his human weakness and his need to rely on God's strength. Now the real preparation could begin.

Make It Personal

Describe a time when you felt humbled.

_____

How did that sense of humility change your actions?

_____

Ask God to reveal areas of your life in which you have accepted the illusion of readiness. Give Him permission to prepare you for what lies ahead.

WHEN

PETER

THOUGHT

THINGS WERE

FALLING APART,

JESUS KNEW

THEY WERE JUST

FALLING INTO PLACE.

Discover the Meaning

After the resurrection Christ graciously restored Peter, preparing him for the next assignment (see John 21:15-17). Although Peter's faith sometimes wavered, it did not fail. In Acts 2 we find Spirit-filled Peter boldly preaching the Word, and thousands were saved. Scripture also reveals that Peter went on to serve as one of the leaders in the Jerusalem church, guiding and strengthening them through some serious trials (see Acts 4:5-20; 11; 15:1-11). The understanding he gained from these experiences is revealed in the Books 1 and 2 Peter.

How do you think humility affected Peter's willingness to serve Jesus?

yes

Carefully read 2 Peter 1:3-11. Which of the following best summarizes Peter's words?
○ Believers should avoid all controversy.
◉ Every believer has a calling and needs to be sure of that calling.
○ Christ does not expect anything from His followers.

Read Ephesians 4:1-3 and 2 Thessalonians 1:11-12. According to these verses, whom has God called?
○ Church leaders   ○ Talented believers   ◉ All believers

Through what are believers able to fulfill their purpose (2 Thess. 1:11)?
◉ God's power   ○ Hard work   ○ Staying physically fit

UNDERSTANDING OUR CALLING

Humility and understanding his calling helped keep Peter's focus on preparing Christ's bride. He recognized his dependence on God's power and acknowledged his life purpose to tell others about Christ. For believers, calling refers not only to our original call to salvation through Christ but also to God's appointment of a purpose for our lives.[6] Part of that purpose is divine partnership–a role directly connected to the church body.

We each have spiritual gifts–supernatural abilities, granted by the Holy Spirit, that empower us to fulfill God's purpose (1 Cor. 12:4-11). Scripture reveals that spiritual gifts are "given for the common good" (v. 7). Surrendering our spiritual gifts, time, and individual talents to our work in the divine partnership leads to the abundant life Jesus spoke of in John 10:10.

God created each of us with a profound need to truly matter that can only be filled when we discover our divine purpose. Many try to fill this need with things, money, relationships, and power; they are left feeling empty and unsatisfied. Only God can give our lives the eternal significance for which we long.

When I left the practice of law to be home with my children, my older daughter was in college and my two youngest children were in elementary school. At first I loved the change, enjoying the opportunity to catch up on housework. But I began to feel lost while the kids were in school. Once the laundry was done and everything was put away, I didn't know what to do with myself. I felt useless and unhappy.

I had no doubt that God wanted me home with my children during that particular season, but I sensed God's purpose for me included something more. As I began to pray about my feelings, God began opening doors for ministry in my church.

Responding to God's call brings genuine joy and deeper meaning to everything. I discovered that partnership with Him extends into all areas of my life. Now I'm blessed with the knowledge that what I'm doing–at home, at church, and wherever He takes me–truly matters. As the years pass, God continues to open exciting new opportunities of ministry in my family, my church, and my community. In Christ, I've found the significance I was searching for. I've found my reason for living.

Make It Personal

Have you discovered God's purpose for you? If so, describe your calling. If not, take time now to follow the ABCs of purpose in the margin.

To prepare for Christ coming / to live a holy life and to get ready

What is God revealing about His purpose for you?

glorify God

How committed are you to using your abilities to attend Christ's bride?

not at all   somewhat   fairly   completely

Remember, a necessary part of becoming ready is admitting and naming the areas you are attempting by your own power. In spite of what the world says, relying on yourself is a formula for failure. You and I will never be ready for Christ's return and will never give our personal best without God's help.

Ask God to take His rightful position as boss in your life. Dedicate your spiritual gifts, time, and talents to Him and the preparation of His beloved bride.

BY HIS POWER

What does 2 Peter 1:3 tell us God has supplied?

Through His Divine Power He has granted everything pertaining to life & godliness

True readiness comes when we humbly rely on God's divine power instead of our abilities. Peter tended to turn to self-reliance. However, he eventually realized he needed God's supernatural power that comes from divine partnership.

Only God can reveal your divine calling and purpose. He does so through His Word, the leadership of the Holy Spirit, and through the prayerful guidance of other believers.

As you seek God's will, consider the following ABCs of purpose.

Acknowledge
God has a purpose for your life. Ask Him to reveal your purpose to you.

To prepare for His coming

Believe in Him who is faithful. God will ultimately accomplish His purpose through you.

Commit to obey whatever God commands.

Decide to allow the Holy Spirit to control every aspect of your life.

Enjoy the blessings of a Spirit-filled life of eternal purpose.

We learned in day 5 of week 2 that God sent the Holy Spirit to live in each believer and provide the power to prepare for Christ's return. Only when we allow the Spirit's power to work in our lives are we truly able to prepare for Christ's return. We must dedicate everything we have—our gifts, time, talents, training, and experiences—to Christ's glory, allowing Him to use our strengths to the fulfillment of His Divine Purpose.

Don't grow discouraged if relinquishing control of your life seems difficult. Recall that humbled Peter learned to allow the Holy Spirit to have control over His life, but only through a spiritual transformation that did not occur overnight.

Only the Holy Spirit can transform our devotion to Christ and His bride from human emotion into supernatural response. The Spirit's power enables us to faithfully and wholeheartedly attend the bride as she prepares for her divine bridegroom's return.

Humbly approach God, asking Him to reveal His individualized purpose for you. Make it your life goal to allow the Holy Spirit to work in you so you may effectively prepare for Christ's return.

ONLY

THE HOLY

SPIRIT

CAN TRANSFORM

OUR DEVOTION

TO CHRIST AND

HIS BRIDE FROM

HUMAN EMOTION

INTO SUPERNATURAL

RESPONSE.

Day Three
Radiating His Character

Have you ever greeted a bride on her wedding day with the exclamation, "You are absolutely glowing!"? Something about a bride's joy and anticipation makes her seem to shine with a timeless radiance that transcends culture. It reflects inner beauty and overwhelming happiness. To better understand the divine partnership, let's consider the spiritual truths reflected in the radiance of Christ's bride.

Biblical Background

Read Isaiah 61:10. Think of the most beautiful bride you've ever seen. Morph that image in your mind to become you standing before Christ in His beautiful garments of salvation. How do you feel about the picture?

loved, adored, radiant beautiful, glorious, glowing, joyful, loving, holiness

The beautiful bridal adornments and the joy associated with them represent God's magnificent gift of salvation. In Revelation 21, the heavenly Jerusalem is also compared to a bride's beauty: "the wife of the Lamb … shone with the glory of God" (vv. 9-10). In Ephesians 5:25-27, Paul hinted at the wedding finery again, describing the church as a "radiant" bride. Each reference points to an obvious glow we commonly call radiance. But what is it that makes the church shine?

MARKED BY LOVE

According to *Webster's Dictionary*, one who is radiant is "marked by love." With that in mind, think of the church as a bride glowing with love for her groom, happily radiating her love for Christ and His love for her. As we'll see, the church's radiance goes beyond surface appearances. Her glorious radiance emanates from the divine transformation taking place within each believer.

Search the Scripture

One of many things that makes Christ's relationship with the church so beautiful is that He transfers His divine radiance to her. His radiance is the manifestation of God's brilliant glory (2 Cor. 4:6). This is not to say that His own glory is depleted in the transfer or that she becomes His divine equal. Instead, this process allows Christ's glory—His character and ways—to dwell in us, becoming our joy, propelling us onward in our preparations, and ultimately drawing others to Him.

Read 2 Corinthians 3:18. According to this passage, we are being transformed into the Lord's ...

    ⊙ image   ◯ veil   ◯ Spirit

How does Jesus resemble His Father? (Col. 1:15 and Heb. 1:3).

> He is the visible image of the invisible God, the firstborn of all creation
>
> Jesus He is the radiance of His God's glory + the exact representation of His nature God's

Christ came to earth as the visible image of invisible God. His actions reflected God's nature. His words reflected God's heart. To be transformed into Christ's image means to become like Him—to reflect His character as He reflects the Father's.

The church's glorious radiance is the outward display of inward holiness that comes when we allow Jesus to forgive and wash away our sins. By receiving Christ's offer of relationship, we become a new creation—made to be like God—truly righteous and holy. Turning our hearts' focus to Him transforms us!

Psalm 34:5 says that those who look to Him become "radiant." Paul compared the magnificent glory Christ gives the church to the glory Moses reflected after his encounter with God (see 2 Cor. 3:7-18). But the glory Moses reflected literally paled in comparison to the glory God has given the church. Why? Moses reflected the glory of an outward encounter with God, a glory that ultimately faded. The church's glory, however, radiates from an inner holiness she receives from her beloved bridegroom: a glory that is "ever-increasing" and will never fade (see 2 Cor. 3:11,18).

Scripture is clear that those who believe in Christ—those who look to Him as Lord and Savior—literally become radiant. But that the divine transfer of glory is not without cost.

According to Ephesians 5:25-27, what did Christ give for church?

    ◯ money   ◯ time   ⊙ Himself   ◯ effort

OUR WORD *GLORY* COMES FROM THE GREEK WORD *DOXA*, WHICH MEANS "OF THE CHARACTER AND WAYS OF GOD AS EXHIBITED THROUGH CHRIST TO AND THROUGH BELIEVERS ... BRIGHTNESS OR SPLENDOR."[7]

One part of Ephesians 5:26 has always seemed odd to me. I wondered what part "cleansing her by the washing with water through the word" had to do with the passage. At one time I wondered if it could be a reference to believer's baptism.

How does what we learned last week about the mikveh shed light on verse 26?

By the word of God, the church is washing of water — cleansed from sin by Christ's blood Symbolic purification —

The church's holiness results not from her own goodness but from the sacrifice of Jesus' body on the cross (see Heb. 10:10; 1 Pet. 2:24). In Ephesians 5 Paul uses wedding imagery to tell us that as the bride had to be cleansed for the wedding, we had to be cleansed from sin. I believe the image suggests that Christ's blood washes us like the mikveh washes the Jewish bride.

God created man in His own image (Gen. 1:26). When sin entered the world, God's image was marred, and we were separated from Him. The intimate relationship God desired was no longer possible. Christ became flesh—the perfect image of God—to reconcile man's relationship with Him (see John 14:6; Col. 1:15,20-22).

Beloved, Jesus suffered and shed His blood to make us holy (Heb. 13:12), but the story does not end there. Jesus died to make us holy for a purpose—so we can experience the joy of deep relationship with Him.

Jesus often spoke of this joy (John 15:11; 16:20,24; 17:13). Even as He endured suffering and death, Jesus focused on the coming joy of restored relationship (Heb. 12:2). I believe the coming wedding celebration and the uninterrupted joy of eternity with those He loved were always on His mind.

Make It Personal

Fill in the blanks with your full name.

Jesus Christ died for *Joy   Allen   Lashrook Turner*

How does it feel to know that Christ gave His life out of His love for you?

Abundantly joyful thankful prayfull tearful, overcome w/ emotion

Answering that question brings tears to my eyes. I am overcome that the divine bridegroom died not just for the church as a whole but for me. I can't help but praise and thank Him for who He is and all He's done. "Thank You, Jesus, for loving me!" "Thank You, Jesus, for saving me!" "Thank You, Jesus, for being my joy!"

I deeply desire to carry this joy so that anyone who sees it will see Christ's glory radiating through me. I desperately want to display this same radiance every day of my life. I'm being been transformed. I want the world to see it!

What purpose do you think radiance might serve?

bring others to Christ — noticeable see the love

A TWOFOLD PURPOSE

The radiance Christ imparted to the church acts like a powerful magnet: It draws and it unifies. Just as we are drawn to the beautiful earthly bride by her radiance, we are pulled to God by the divine bride's glorious radiance. Christ's beauty and incredible love shows as the church loves Him, lives Him, and leads others to Him.

One young woman recently shared a story that illustrates this well. "I'll never forget Layla," she explained as her eyes sparkled with a treasured memory. "We met in high school and became fast friends. But while we got along well and always enjoyed one another's company, we just couldn't see eye-to-eye on the God issue.

"At first, I often talked to her about Jesus, but when I sensed that it made her uncomfortable, I changed tactics. I made up my mind to be the best friend I could be to her. I became a listener. A shoulder to cry on. I asked God to minister to her through me. To shine through my actions.

"Many months later, Layla told me something that changed my life. 'You radiate love,' she said. With happy tears rolling down my chin, I enthusiastically thanked her before explaining that the radiant love she saw in me came from the Lord."

Have you encountered someone who radiated God's love? If so, explain.

Diane, Peggy, Cheri, & Alison   dpac   Adrian Rogers

Discover the Meaning

Though many of us may not hear such confirmation, those we encounter should definitely see evidence of Christ's radiance working in the church and in our lives. Jesus gave His glory so believers could become an appealing community of faith—a family whose existence demonstrates God's amazing love (John 17:22-23).

Read Ephesians 3:16-19. In Paul's prayer for the Ephesians, what insights do you see into how God accomplishes His plan to work through the church?

Strengthen the church w/ power through His Spirit in the inner man so that Christ may dwell in their hearts through faith + be grounded & rooted in love.

I wish I could be there to hear your observations. I hope you included that by joining other believers in community we gain a greater grasp of Christ's love for us.

Make It Personal

Believers become part of a community that brings glory to God—a family designed to point others to Him. God accomplishes His plan for the church as individual believers, established in His love, join together to receive the fullness of His glory.

God intentionally created us to need one another (1 Cor. 12:12-27). Our need for each other is critical to God's plan for the church and our call to attend Christ's bride.

How does our God-given need for one another relate to our call to attend the bride of Christ?

_____

How do other believers impact your understanding of God's love?

When they are radiant when talking about Jesus and His love, my kinsman Redeemer

The bride of Christ's glorious radiance serves a divine purpose—drawing others to God and further unifying the church. Glory, glory hallelujah!

Day Four
Transformed by Righteousness

If you've ever had the privilege of helping a bride-to-be shop for her wedding dress, you know an amazing transformation takes place when a young woman slips into her bridal gown. Gone is the little girl who played dress up in her mother's closet. Gone is the average woman. A vision in white suddenly resembles a fairy tale princess. Radiating confidence and excitement, she is transformed.

Today we consider how God transfigures the church into a unified, holy bride. That insight will guide us to understand our part in preparing for Christ's return.

Biblical Background

Christ's bride is a work in progress. We do not yet see the complete, perfected church. When Christ returns, the transformation will be complete, and we'll finally fix our eyes upon the fully prepared, radiant church.

Today's church is still preparing, continuing the process of divine transformation (1 Cor. 3:18). "The church today is not perfect;" one commentator explains, "it has spots and wrinkles. Spots are caused by defilement on the outside, while wrinkles are caused by decay on the inside."[8] Sin, hypocrisy, and even the presence of unsaved people affect the condition of today's church.

We joyfully welcome the unsaved, hoping they will receive Christ and become a part of the community of believers. Until they do, however, their presence does not contribute to the church's perfection. Only those who have received Christ are being made perfect (Heb. 10:14), and all of us have room for improvement.

OUR NEED FOR EACH OTHER IS CRITICAL TO GOD'S PLAN FOR THE CHURCH AND OUR CALL TO ATTEND CHRIST'S BRIDE.

When Christ returns, the unsaved—those who do not truly know Him—will be cut off from the bride (see Matt. 22:10-14). Then, in the twinkling of an eye, the bride will be fully transformed and presented to Christ without blemish (see 1 Cor. 15:51-52). She will be perfected as "a radiant church, without stain or wrinkle or any other blemish, but holy and blameless" (Eph. 5:27).

Let's take a closer look at this divine transformation process.

THE GOWN OF RIGHTEOUSNESS

When most of us consider the transformation process that turns a young woman into a bride, one of the first things that comes to mind is her beautiful bridal gown. Recall that an important part of the ancient Jewish bride's preparation during the betrothal period included sewing her wedding garments. These were special garments befitting of the joyous occasions to come (see Ps. 45:13-14).

Search the Scripture

Describe the clothes of Christ's transformed bride (Rev. 19:8).

fine linen, bright & clean

What does the fine linen represent? *# Ag to the glory of God them*

○ A new life   ● The righteous acts of saints   ○ The bride's readiness

Read Isaiah 64:6. To what are man's righteous acts compared?

like filthy garments

I know what you are thinking. *How can the bride of Christ's fine linen represent the righteous acts of saints if man's righteous acts are "as filthy rags"?* The answer lies in the divine partnership we studied on day 1. Our self-righteous acts and efforts to be good are filthy rags—a material completely unfit for a wedding garment. Divine partnership with God, however, allows us to depend on God's righteousness rather than our own. His righteousness is always bright and clean like fine linen—the perfect material for a glorious wedding gown!

Revelation 19:8 clearly states that Christ's bride does not earn or make the glorious gown of righteousness. It is *given* to her. The gown is God's gracious gift.

According to Romans 3:23, why did we need God's righteousness?

all have sinned & fall short of the glory of God

Read 2 Corinthians 5:21. How do we become the righteousness of God?

God made (who knew know sin Jesus) became sin on our behalf so that we might become the righteousness of God in Him Jesus

Jesus took our place on the cross

Scripture says that God's righteousness is available to all who believe in Christ (Rom. 3:22). The transformation of Christ's bride begins with the righteous garment of salvation He died to give her, and it will be completed at the marriage supper of the Lamb when she receives the wedding garment. Our attempts at righteousness will never be good enough to accomplish God's purpose for our lives, but God graciously provided a way for His righteousness to come to us through Christ. All who receive Christ are given the gift of God's righteousness—and one day we will wear the robes that show it.

THE CIRCLE OF LOVE

God's righteousness transforms the church. She is assured of her wedding garment, but Christ's bride should desire to present herself delightful, chaste, and lovable. She must set out to please Him in all that she does, conforming to His loving will and divine plan. The supernatural power of Christ's love for her makes this possible.

Search the Scripture

What did Jesus say, is the greatest commandment (Matt. 22:34-40)?

You shall love the LORD your GOD w/ all your heart + w/ all your soul, + w/ all your mind.

And the second? *You shall love your neighbor as yourself.*

Read 1 John 4:7-21. Write the number of the verse(s) beside each statement that explains how we are able to love God.

11 cooperate with God to love others
14 testify to Christ
16 receive and rest in His sacrifice
13 possess His Spirit
19 acknowledge God first loved us

Jesus summed up God's commands in one word: love. First, we love God, and His love teaches us to love others. Second, we love others as He commands, allowing Him to love through us. Our obedience to these great commands transforms us and the church into an increasingly lovely bride. You may have answered the activity in a variety of ways, but the passage points to all these ways we can love God.

Discover the Meaning

The love God provides leads to the unity of the church and the salvation of the lost. It also allows the depth of spiritual insight necessary for remaining pure and blameless until Christ returns.

Let's connect these truths with those we learned yesterday. God's love offers righteousness through salvation and empowers us to be a community of faith. Our participation in the community of faith enables us to more fully comprehend His infinite love, leading to the spiritual insight (maturity) needed to remain holy and righteous. The increasing holiness of believers and the church results in a greater display of God's visible radiant glory. As God is lifted up and made more visible, He will draw all men to Himself (John 12:32). This results in the salvation of the lost, further expanding the circle of God's eternal love. Only God's righteousness can transform us into the lovely, radiant bride of Christ.

Make It Personal

Consider your relationship with God, other believers, and those who do not know Christ. Where do you find yourself in the circle of God's love?

- ○ I need to receive God's love by receiving His great salvation.
- ○ I need to become a part of the community of faith.
- ○ I am receiving greater understanding of God's love through fellowship with other believers.
- ● I am learning that greater understanding of God's love leads to spiritual insight and loving service to others.
- ○ As a result of God's love and my relationship with other believers, I am growing in holiness, and reflecting God's radiant glory more.

Where would you like to be?

Greater Holiness & Visible Radiant Glory of God

Choose the statement that best describes your relationship with God.

- ○ My relationship with God has become broken and stagnant. I'm not moving forward in the circle of His love.
- ● I am moving forward in the circle of love. Our relationship is growing.

If you answered that your relationship is broken, mark the spot where the circle has broken. Consider what God would have you do to restore relationship with Him.

As we conclude, take a moment to look over your answers. How is your present situation affecting your responsibilities to attend the bride of Christ with steadfast devotion?

Not physically attending a church service on ~~mission evangelizing~~ _Sunday a.m._

Beloved, attending Christ's bride begins and ends with love. I pray that we will each grow in love for Him as we daily abound in His unfailing love for us!

Day Five
Focused on Him

I keep a small book on a table in our living room that contains pictures of my daughter Amber's wedding. Even now, years after the big event, we take great pleasure in looking at them and sharing the joy of that special time with others. Wedding pictures capture unique moments in time and remind us of treasured experiences.

I'm fond of most wedding photos, especially my daughter's, but I'm particularly drawn to the portrait of a Jewish wedding scene that hangs in my home. As I gaze at it, I'm touched by the bride's radiance. But I am most moved by her apparent focus. Her eyes are fixed on the object of her affection: the bridegroom. Placing her hope in his promise to love and provide for her, she pledges her allegiance to him. Together the two will face life's ups and downs, blessings and tragedies, hand-in-hand. Their relationship is a sacred partnership.

THE SOURCE OF HOPE

Biblical Background

During the ancient Jewish betrothal separation, the bride placed all hope in the return of her beloved bridegroom. His expected return formed the basis of everything she was and did during this time of preparation. Being ready for his return became her all-consuming life purpose. If he did not return, everything she had devoted herself to would be meaningless, all her labor would have been in vain, and her future would be hopelessly uncertain.

Search the Scripture

Like the betrothed Jewish bride of ancient times, Christ's bride also eagerly awaits the return of her beloved bridegroom. The hope she places in Him and her focus on His return are essential to the successful completion of the church's preparation.

Hope in Christ is the heartbeat of every believer and of the church. Our living hope in Him and in His commitment to fulfilling His promises defines us. It should motivate all we do. The Lord promised to provide us salvation, and He lovingly kept His promise. He promised us the indwelling Holy Spirit to guide and empower us, and He sent Him. Jesus Christ promised He would return, and He will. This is our "blessed hope" (Titus 2:13). Beloved, "no matter how many promises God has made, they are 'Yes' in Christ" (2 Cor. 1:20).

Learn to cling to His promises! "He who promised is faithful" (Heb. 10:23).

By what "power" are we able to "overflow with hope" (Rom. 15:13)?

by the power of the Holy Spirit

Read Romans 5:5-8. Why does our hope in Christ not disappoint us?
- ○ Because we are ungodly
- ◉ Because God's love has been poured into our hearts
- ○ Because we are good people who don't deserve disappointment

Make It Personal

Only God is 100 percent reliable. Hold on to your hope in Him! The Lord is bound to His promises; whatever He says He will do, He will do. Be inspired by Paul's prayer that the church in Rome not just have hope, but "overflow with hope" (Rom. 15:13)! This marvelous living hope keeps us focused on Christ, stirring expectation of the divine bridegroom's impending return.

Through the many ups and downs of my life, only Christ has remained firm and secure. In days of despair He has been my hope. Dear friend, others have failed me. No doubt they have failed you. Jesus is different. He will not disappoint. Our hope in Him is "an anchor for the soul, firm and secure" (Heb. 6:19). We can trust Him!

FAITHFULLY HIS

When the Jewish bride promised to faithfully remain set apart during the betrothal separation, she promised to stay focused on her beloved and the preparations for his return. This focused commitment produced faithfulness, and it also sent a clear message to any potential suitors: "I belong to my bridegroom and no other. My allegiance belongs to him." Likewise, the church is to remain pure and holy, faithfully set apart for Christ (2 Cor. 11:2). Scripture admonishes us to "fix our eyes on Jesus, the author and perfecter of our faith" (Heb. 12:2). Staying focused on Christ and the preparations for His return helps us remain faithful to Him and our vital mission.

HOPE IN

CHRIST

IS THE

HEARTBEAT

OF EVERY BELIEVER

AND OF THE

CHURCH.

According to 1 Thessalonians 5:23-24, how are we able to remain holy?

[handwritten: Through God's power. He will preserve my Spirit + Soul + body w/o (God is faithful) blame @ the coming of my I am to obediently cooperate Lord Jesus Christ access to my life, w/ God to allow Him full]

[handwritten left margin: Be Christlike through the power of God]

The church can neither make herself holy nor remain holy in her own strength. Only God's mighty power can sanctify or purify the church, presenting her to Christ as a pure virgin bride, holy and blameless. This is the work of the divine partnership, and it requires us to obediently cooperate with God, allowing Him full access to our lives and His church (Heb. 12:10-11).

Christ's bride must choose between faith in herself and faith in her beloved. Consider for a moment the difference between self-centered faith and Christ-centered faith. List and compare the results of faith in self and faith in Christ.

Faith in Self	Faith in Christ
focused on the world	*focused on Jesus*
prideful	*holiness*
	assurance
arrogant	*thankfulness*
	generous
hypocritical	*sharing*
materialistic	*helpful + kind*
insecure hopelessness	*thoughtful loving + joyful*
fearful	*hopeful*

A self-centered individual places her faith in her own performance and abilities, all the while wondering if she is being holy enough. *I'm going to church three times a week, giving to the church's food pantry, and I try not to lie or think bad thoughts* she might tell herself, before dissolving into tears because she's afraid God may expect more. Deep down she knows she is incapable of pleasing God through her efforts alone. Her self-centered faith leads to insecurity, fear, and overwhelming hopelessness.

A Christ-centered individual, on the other hand, places her faith in Jesus and His power to make and keep her holy. She sees her shortcomings as opportunities to showcase His divine strength. This believer knows she messes up sometimes, but she is always quick to confess her downfalls to God and to ask for His guidance. Keeping her attention focused on Jesus, she experiences assurance, joy, and hope.

Discover the Meaning

Understand that remaining faithfully holy is an ongoing process that will not end until Christ returns (1 Thess. 5:23-24). We accomplish continued holiness as individual believers and the church obediently live pure lives through God's power. We must surrender to God, allowing the Holy Spirit to control each part of our lives.

Giving up control has never been easy for me. For example, when Katie and Taylor were young, I prepared a detailed daily schedule for their caregiver who came into our home. The schedule varied slightly from day to day, but included when to eat, when to nap, and when to play. I also made a form for her to fill out each afternoon reporting the details of my children's day.

Yes, I'm a person who likes to be in charge! Unfortunately, that tendency sometimes leaves me focused on myself instead of the bridegroom. But God is patient and daily provides the grace I need to give up control to His Spirit. As I yield to Him, He empowers me to do and be what He has called me to do and be (Heb. 13:20-21). The more control I give to God, the more of the Spirit's power I experience (see Rom. 8). I find freedom and peace in letting go.

His will

Make It Personal

The church and individual believers should, like a bride focused on her husband-to-be, shield themselves from the temptation to seek another. We must neither abandon our commitment to live holy lives nor allow the world to defile the church and her members. Just remembering the promise to remain holy is not enough, however. We must actively remain in God's power to maintain holiness.

The church must choose between faith in self or faith in Jesus. We are each individually responsible for making that choice. Beloved, will you depend on yourself—continually taking your own spiritual temperature to determine if you are holy enough? Or will you put your full confidence in Christ—warming yourself at His fire and enjoying the comfort of knowing His power is at work in you?

No matter what others may say or do, you can be sure that Christ will return. Until then, may He find us faithfully set apart and focused on Him alone.

Where do you stand regarding a holy life focused on Christ?
- ❍ I have not yet placed my hope in Christ.
- ❍ I'm not pursuing a life of holiness at this time.
- ❍ My hope is in myself and my resources.
- ❍ I want to put all my hope and focus on Christ.
- ❍ I'm learning to keep my focus fixed on Christ and my hope in Him.
- ❍ I'm trying to live a holy life, but sometimes I rely on my own power.
- ◉ I'm learning to rely on God's power to keep my hope in Christ alone and to live a holy life.

What threatens to pull you away from your hope in Christ's return?

_____

Think for a moment about the connection between our hope in Christ and our call to attend His bride with steadfast devotion. How might your level of hope in the bridegroom's return affect your church?

_____

Beloved, people will disappoint us. The world will try to pull us away from our love. We must be certain of where we have placed our hope.

Jesus is coming! Live in anticipation of that glorious moment!

Meet 7/11/2011

Ornaments of Grace

4

As a girl, I loved to play dress up! What a thrill to rummage through Mom's closet and jewelry chest! I'd sped hours preparing for imaginary social engagements. How exhilarating to see things finally coming together as I preened in front of the mirror! To me it didn't matter that my red high heels were too big or that my pink pearl necklace was obviously broken and dangling down to my knees. Any such flaws instantly disappeared as I excitedly announced to the mirror, "I'm ready!"

The church received an invitation to the divine wedding feast and a direct command to make herself ready for Christ's return. This reality brings a sense of urgency that at times can feel overwhelming. I believe, however, that God intended this time of challenging readiness to also be one of extraordinary joy. As we collectively adorn Christ's bride with spiritual ornaments, we should find even more delight in the preparation process than anxious, bright-eyed little girls find in selecting just the right broach and scarf to complement their tea party ensembles.

This week as we examine the church's purposeful preparations for her bridegroom's return, I pray you will discover a new appreciation for the work of the church. May you experience fresh joy and excitement as we look forward to the moment when the Father declares the time has come—Christ's bride is ready.

Day One
Making Herself Ready

Last week we explored the mysteries of the divine partnership between God and man—a relationship comprised of God the master and us as willing servants. Remember that God does not need our help but rather allows us to join Him for our benefit. What a privilege to partner with Him as we prepare for Christ's coming!

This week we'll seek to better understand the church's call to make herself ready. We'll take a detailed look at the specific tasks for which she is responsible. Closely examining the four primary responsibilities of the church during this time of preparation, we'll consider how each prepares the bride for Christ's return. And we'll take a look at just how important it is that we as believers work together.

ADORNING THE BRIDE

Biblical Background

Before we can understand the specific spiritual ornaments, we need to explore the concept of adorning the bride. The Bible describes a fully prepared bride as beautifully "adorned" for her husband (Rev. 21:2).

The word translated "adorned" in Revelation 21 is *kosmeo*, a verb meaning, "to put in order, arrange, make ready, prepare."[1] Quite literally, the beautifully adorned bride is one made ready to meet her groom. We've seen it's the duty of each believer to help her prepare. We fulfill our role as attendants to Christ's bride through this service. You attend, I attend, and together we adorn the bride of Christ. Adornment describes our collective work as we join together as a community of servants.

Imagine we have been commissioned to make an intricate quilt. Because we each have some—though no one has all—of the talents necessary, we must work together. While we are individually responsible for certain tasks, we collaborate closely on several key sections to complete the project.

Periodically we meet, delighting over the progress we're making, teaching one another new sewing tips we've learned, and enjoying one another's company. In the meantime, I work at home cutting triangles and blocks, while you are hard at work on a special, scalloped border. Each time we get together, we check the project specifications to make sure we are on track and then piece our work into place.

The actions you and I do on our own are like the individual responsibility to attend the bride. Our joint effort is much like the collective responsibility to adorn her. Whether creating a quilt or joining forces to prepare Christ's bride, cooperation produces a complete and beautiful work of art—a masterpiece we could never finish alone.

As we study together this week, keep in mind that we prepare the bride primarily through divine partnership with God. He designed this partnership to require us to willingly cooperate with Him and other believers to effectively make ready for the bridegroom's coming.

ADORNMENT

DESCRIBES OUR

COLLECTIVE WORK

AS A COMMUNITY

OF SERVANTS.

What advantages does teamwork have over solitary efforts?

Combine our different talents

What teamwork is needed to prepare a modern bride for her wedding?

PREPARING HER HEART

Search the Scripture

A modern bride's preparations illustrate the concept of adorning the church, but don't rely too heavily on that image as we look at spiritual adornment. Unlike modern brides who focus on physical appearance, Christ's bride is collectively called to focus on the preparation of her heart. Christ is concerned with *inner* beauty. Scripture says, " 'The LORD does not look at the things man looks at. Man looks at the outward appearance, but the LORD looks at the heart' " (1 Sam. 16:7).

Peter illustrates the distinction between inner and outer adornment. In the margin, underline the external adornments and circle the internal.

How might a gentle and quiet spirit reflect spiritual transformation?

Spiritual adornment begins on the inside and results in external change. In Titus 2:9-10, Paul illustrated the attractiveness of inner adornment by a slave's attitude toward his owner. The servant's godly attitude toward his master attracts the master to Christ. Likewise, the spiritually adorned church radiates the glory of God's amazing grace, which attracts the world to Jesus.

Make It Personal

Last week we discussed how individual believers radiate Christ's love through their attitudes and actions. With that in mind, what qualities do you think God desires to see in the heart of the church as a whole? (Check all that apply.)

● love	● kindness	● helpfulness	● perseverance
● faithfulness	● devotion	● self-control	● generosity
○ self-interest	○ greed	○ hate	● peace
● gentleness	○ fear	○ prejudice	● joy

Proverbs 1:7 the fear of the Lord is beginning of the knowledge

Circle those that are obviously part of your church's spiritual adornment.

"YOUR BEAUTY **SHOULD NOT** COME FROM **OUTWARD ADORNMENT,** *such as braided hair and the wearing of gold jewelry and fine clothes. Instead, it should be that of your* **INNER SELF,** THE UNFADING BEAUTY OF A GENTLE AND QUIET SPIRIT, *which is of great worth in God's sight.*

1 PETER 3:3-4

How might these qualities attract to God those who don't attend church?

_____

SPECIFIC ORNAMENTS OF GRACE

Biblical Background

The word _ornament_ comes from the root word "adorned," and means "a quality … conferring grace or honor."[2] In ancient times, the Jewish bride's wedding attire included beautiful handmade ornaments either sewn on her wedding garment or worn separately. For instance, Jeremiah 2:32 mentions jewelry and a wedding sash. These ornaments were an important part of a woman's preparation for the wedding celebration and a source of great delight as she awaited her beloved's return.

Just as a Jewish bride arrayed herself in ornaments, Christ's bride is to put on spiritual ornaments–specific spiritual adornments that reflect the grace and honor God has bestowed on the church. Each of these visible extensions of God's amazing grace reveals a unique aspect of His grace at work through the divine partnership.

The church's ornaments of grace represent God's work in and through her in four primary areas: worship, instruction, fellowship, and evangelism. These beautiful ornaments are carefully interwoven with the powerful thread of unceasing prayer–a factor critical to the success of each. The acronym WIFE helps me to remember the specific ornaments.

Worship
instruction
fellowship
Evangelism

Search the Scripture

Today we'll define the ornaments of grace. Throughout the week we'll examine each. As we work, consider that helping prepare the bride's ornaments of grace is one way we demonstrate our personal devotion to Christ. Remember, we cannot devotedly serve and prepare the bride without active involvement in the life of the church. This week's discussion will take "involvement" to a whole new level.

Worship
  Read Jeremiah 2:32 in the margin.
 True worship acknowledges God, giving Him first place. In Jeremiah 2:32, God contrasts the Israelites' failure to acknowledge Him with the bride's careful remembrance of her wedding ornaments. Just as the Jewish bride treasured her wedding garments, we must continually treasure God's rightful place in our lives.
Instruction
  Read Proverbs 1:8-9.
Receiving instruction grows us in things of the Lord, leading to our spiritual maturity. Instruction includes teaching through words and actions, as well as encouragement and admonition. Proverbs describes wise instruction as "an ornament of grace" (KJV) to those who listen and obey.
Fellowship

For further study on the important difference between inner and outer adornment, consider Matthew 23:29-32 and Luke 21:5-6.

"Does a maiden **FORGET** _her jewelry, a bride her wedding ornaments?_ YET MY PEOPLE HAVE **FORGOTTEN ME.**_"_ JEREMIAH 2:32

Believers
special love relationship
Appreciate fellowship w/ her

Read Ezekiel 16:8-14. According to verses 11 and 12, what did God do for Israel and why do you think He did it?

Adorned w/ ornaments, put bracelets on hands + a necklace around neck. Ring in nostril, earrings in ears + a beautiful crown on head.

Believers share fellowship, a special love relationship, with God and one another. This passage reveals God's active pursuit of relationship with His people, remarkably describing the love relationship through imagery of the marriage experience. In preparing Israel to be a beautiful bride, God adorns her with ornaments. These ornaments symbolize God's love for her and the special relationship they shared. In the same way, the fellowship of believers with God and one another is an ornament of grace preparing the bride for the return of her groom.

Evangelism
Read Isaiah 49:16-18.

Evangelism is our response to Christ's command to tell others about the salvation God provides. Isaiah 49:18 describes God's victory over Israel's enemy as an ornament put on a bride. The church is engaged in a battle for souls (Eph. 6:12). Victory is ensured because God has graciously provided redemption for all who believe in Christ. Yet the battle continues. Until Jesus returns, the church is called to spread the victorious news that Jesus lovingly gave His life and powerfully rose again as payment for the world's sins. As the church shares the message of salvation, Satan's defeat is confirmed, and the bride is further prepared for her groom's coming.

Write the words of the acronym WIFE and a brief explanation for each in your own words. *God + His Kingdom are first because they are the all-prevailing influences that prevail + control all that we think, and are and do.*

W orship. Give God first place. Glorify (Praise) Him

I Bible Study discipline - Sermons - Teaching Instruction - allowing God's authority over all my life.

F ellowship w/ other believers

E vangelism - Missions - outreach testify about Jesus + the Gospel

Discover the Meaning

The early church passionately cultivated these ornaments of grace through the power of the Holy Spirit, combined with the thread of unceasing prayer. God's grace and power were clearly evident as they worshiped, received instruction, fellowshipped together, and testified about Jesus (Acts 2:42-47). Today the church must continue actively and passionately pursuing the refinement of her ornaments of grace because each, as we'll see, plays a key role in making us ready.

"LIFT UP YOUR
EYES AND
LOOK
AROUND;
*all your sons gather and
come to you. As surely as
I live," declares the Lord,
"you will wear them as*
ORNAMENTS;
YOU WILL PUT THEM
ON, LIKE A BRIDE."
ISAIAH 49:18

Make It Personal

Beloved, as I study the church's ornaments of grace, I'm moved by the early church's uninhibited dependence on God. Recognizing her desperate need for Christ, the church fervently prayed and depended on Him to answer (Acts 4:23-31). She faithfully relied on the Holy Spirit to guide and direct her.

My heart's desire is that today's churches rediscover our deep dependence on God, prayerfully seeking ways to further our readiness for Christ's return. Friend, we cannot neglect our ornaments of grace. Worship is vital to our preparation. Instruction is vital to our growth, fellowship is vital to our future, and evangelism is the heart of all we believe.

Which ornament of grace does your local church best display?
○ worship ○ instruction ○ fellowship ○ evangelism

Which ornament is she most likely to neglect?

_____

How might your church polish the ornament you identified?

_____

Consider your own walk. How does seeing yourself attending the bride of Christ differ from seeing yourself just going to or participating in an organization called the church?

Pray & obey
_____

_____

Don't grow discouraged if you feel that both you and your local church fall short in one or two of those areas. We've learned that the beautifully adorned bride of Christ is the fully prepared church, but we are completely incapable of preparing the bride on our own. Remember, partnership with God is critical to our success. Effectively preparing for Christ's return requires that we fall to our knees in prayer and then obediently respond to the Spirit's direction.

Pause and pray. Ask God to help you see how your church needs to grow spiritually. Expectantly listen for His direction, then record your thoughts. Remember, today's church is imperfect. Only through God's transforming power will she ever be all He intends her to be.

_____

_____

_____

Day Two
Adorning Through Worship

Today we begin our detailed examination of the church's ornaments of grace, with a focus on worship. Although each ornament applies to each believer, the ornaments affect the collective church as she prepares for her beloved bridegroom's return. As we work, ask yourself how each ornament contributes to the bride's preparation. Note your thoughts in the margins.

UNDERSTANDING WORSHIP

What comes to your mind when you hear the word worship?

hymns, praise, liturgical service

I'm guessing our responses to that question vary widely. Worship is a term frequently used yet rarely defined. Perhaps that's because the Bible does not specifically define it. We won't try to pack worship into a concise definition. Instead, I want to expand our understanding of true worship. I hope you'll find the topic as exciting as I do!

Biblical Background

WORSHIP
IS A RESPONSE
TO THE TRUTH
OF WHO GOD IS.

For many years, I defined worship as religious music or a service I attended. Each time I read the word *worship* in Scripture, I mentally applied the verse to a church service. But as I've grown in the Lord, I've learned that true worship—whether it happens in a sanctuary or a living room, a mountaintop or a deathbed—is not defined by a style of music or an order of service. Worship is a response to the truth of who God is.

Though Scripture does not define worship, it is filled with examples of it. We find the common thread of man's response to God's grandeur, goodness, love, and mercy. We are designed to respond to God, but you know from experience how our sinful nature is disinclined to put anything above self. When I am controlled by the flesh, everything is about me, and nothing is more important than what I want. Only when we acknowledge God do we truly worship Him. We must get past ourselves—our personal desires, distractions, and concerns—to do that.

The following verses illustrate various ways people respond to God.
Match each Scripture with the specific worship offering it describes.

A 2 Chronicles 29:28-29   (a) singing and blowing trumpets
C Nehemiah 9:3-6   (b) bowing down, kneeling
d Psalm 34:1-3   (c) blessing the Lord and crying out to Him
B Psalm 95:1-7   (d) verbal praise
E Psalm 100   (e) serving with gladness

Explain what goes through your mind as you worship.

Be thankful and say so. Thank God for every blessing I can think of.

What about God makes you want to praise Him?

He is my hope + my power (as I am indwelt by the Holy Spirit)
He is my Creator, my Redeemer, and my Restorer.
He is the bridegroom who will return for His bride,
the church (all believers) →

Search the Scripture

God is Creator, Redeemer, and Restorer. He is the author of our destinies and the hope of our future. God is worthy of wholehearted praise. But though we may sing to Him until our throats are sore or thank Him for every wonderful thing He has done in our lives, on our own we are incapable of the worship God demands. Only by the power of God's Spirit can we truly worship Him. Only He can transform us into people holy and pleasing to Him as we honor Him not just with our lips but with the condition of our hearts (Mark 7:6).

Because of our sinful nature, worship–no matter how well intended–is in vain apart from the Holy Spirit (John 4:24; Rom. 8:5-8; Phil. 3:3). Thankfully, there is a way to gauge the sincerity and value of our worship.

I'm reminded of how patiently Jesus explained the Holy Spirit to His followers. On one occasion, He compared the often unseen work of the Spirit to the wind (John 3:8). Like the wind, the activity of the Spirit may be invisible to mortal eyes, but the results are more obvious. This same principle applies to the spiritual discipline of worship. While it may be difficult to determine whether worship is genuine, the results of true worship are easily observed.

Read Romans 12:1-2. What, according to verse 2, is the result of genuine worship?
- ○ a lasting feeling of happiness
- ○ conviction of sin
- ● transformation by the renewing our minds
- ○ material blessings and easier lives

learn to think differently

Discover the Meaning

True worship *transforms us*. As we cooperate with God, He renews our minds, taking our thoughts off life's distractions and refocusing our attention on His goodness. As believers unite in genuine worship, the church is renewed and further transformed into Christ's radiant bride. The more the church allows God to transform her, the more she can discern His good, pleasing, and perfect will (Rom. 12:2).

With this in mind, explain how worship points others to Christ.

Changes us from inside out by learning to think differently, giving God all the glory.

> [Jesus said,]
> "Isaiah was right …
> **HYPOCRITES** …
> honor me with their
> **LIPS,** but their
> **HEARTS** are far
> from me."
> **MARK 7:6**

A WORSHIP CONTROVERSY

Search the Scripture

Worship is designed to give God glory and to keep our hearts focused on Him. The transformation resulting from genuine worship reveals more of Christ and His glorious grace to the world. Ironically, throughout history we have wrestled with issues concerning worship's form. I'm reminded of the time King David "danced" before the Lord but received harsh criticism from his own wife (see 2 Sam. 6:14-16, 20-21). Later, in questioning the rigid, ritualistic practices of the Pharisees, Jesus taught that God is more interested in the substance of worship than in its form (Mark 7:1-9).

What controversy concerning worship appears in John 4:19-24?

You worship what you do not know.

Why, according to verse 24, must we worship "in spirit and in truth"?

God is Spirit + worship is all about God

Jesus did not take sides in this worship controversy. Instead, He focused on the heart of the issue: the essence of true worship. Worship is all about God and focusing completely on Him. Yet our own need to be right can impair our ability to understand God's heart concerning worship.

Music has always been an important aspect of corporate worship. Unfortunately, it has also been the catalyst for many arguments within the church body. Today some churches struggle with issues of worship style. I once read an article that referred to such controversies as "worship wars."

How does your church respond to controversies over worship styles?

_____

Make It Personal

Worship is for neither human entertainment nor enjoyment but God's pleasure. Corporate worship is meant to glorify Him, thanking Him for who He is and what He has done. Yet many churches spend a lot of time and energy debating personal preferences. Remember that true worship brings hearts near to God (Ps. 24:3-6). He evaluates our worship from the inside out—beginning with the condition of our hearts. I'm not suggesting that having a worship preference is wrong, but placing too much importance on our personal preferences is unwise.

Friend, worship wars begin when individuals allow their own preferences to distract them from worshiping in spirit and in truth. Don't allow the fact that you prefer contemporary music to hymns or organ accompaniment to keyboards affect your willingness to worship in your church.

Have you ever heard about or participated in a worship war? If so, explain. Please be careful to speak kindly and not use names.

_____

How do your attitudes and actions affect your church's worship?

_____

_____

Worship is the responsibility and privilege of each individual within the church.
• Our attitudes and actions effect the quality of worship of the church.
• Worship is an ornament of God's grace, not our works.
• True worship can only be experienced through the grace and power of God.
• The fruit of Spirit-led worship is obedience: putting God's principles into practice.
• Authentic worship leads to holiness, preparing Christ's bride for His return.

So, come let us worship the Lord together and declare, "Not to us, O LORD, not to us but to your name be the glory, because of your love and faithfulness" (Ps. 115:1). Amen!

Day Three
Adorning Through Instruction

Yesterday we explored worship, the first ornament of grace to adorn Christ's bride. Now we'll look at a second ornament: instruction. Few of us like instruction. We want to be independent and think ourselves capable of making decisions on our own. My youngest daughter, Katie, illustrates this well. Always independent, her first complete sentence was, "I'll do it myself!"

Over the years Katie has used that sentence in many settings and situations, but I've heard it most often in our kitchen. Katie loves to cook, but she wants to cook Katie's way. I'm not exaggerating when I tell you that my sweet, lovable child turns into a tyrant as she assembles a casserole or cake. Her independence sometimes makes teaching her difficult and preparing a meal with her a real challenge. But as Katie becomes older, she grows wiser. While she still dislikes instruction, she is beginning to see its benefits. She recently called me from her college apartment to find out how to prepare a roast in a slow cooker!

Perhaps you're inclined to avoid instruction, approaching life with a hearty, "I'll do it myself!" Or, like Katie, your aversion to instruction may be most obvious in a certain area of your life. Perhaps you have even declared certain areas "off limits" to outside input or guidance. Friend, we all have things we want to do our own way. But as Christians, we must be willing to receive God's instruction, allowing Him authority over every aspect of our lives.

UNDERSTANDING INSTRUCTION

Biblical Background

The Hebrew word often translated "instruction" in the Old Testament is *musar*, which means "discipline … it teaches how to live correctly in the fear of the Lord, so that the wise man learns his lesson before temptation and testing."[3] The Septuagint, or Greek translation of the Old Testament, uses *paideia* in place of the Hebrew word *musar*. *Paideia* is used in the New Testament as well and means "the whole training and education of children (which relates to cultivation of mind and morals)."[4] Both definitions suggest life training.

> **To what do Ephesians 4:14 and 1 Peter 2:2 compare new believers?**
>
> *Children + newborn babies*

Both Paul and Peter compared new believers to children or newborn babies. This illustrates a believer's need to grow in the things of God, continuously learning more about Him. Such learning leads to spiritual maturity, a key factor in effectively attending Christ's bride. Whether you are a new believer or you accepted Christ many years ago, you need continual instruction to grow spiritually. We all do.

Search the Scripture

The early church was rooted in God's Word. The believers in Berea carefully checked Paul's teaching against Scripture. The early church depended on God's Word to reveal truth and guide them in how to serve the Lord. They understood Scripture as a book of instruction and revered it as such.

> **The verses below use the Hebrew word *musar*. Surely these passages inspired the early church! Summarize what each says about instruction.**
>
> Proverbs 3:11-12 *Do not reject the discipline of the Lord or loathe His reproof. The Lord will reproof those He loves just as a father corrects his child whom He loves.*
>
> Proverbs 4:13 *Take hold of instruction, do not let go. Guard her, for she is your life.*
>
> Proverbs 23:12 *Apply your heart to discipline. And your ears to the words of knowledge.*

Apply God's words to our lives

Recall that the Hebrew word for instruction is sometimes referred to as discipline, a term that comes from the word disciple.[5] Discipleship (becoming a disciple) is a process through which we learn to apply God's Word to our lives. Remember, Jesus taught by example that we are to incorporate God's truth into every aspect of life.

Discipleship takes many forms including teaching, admonishing, encouraging, and equipping, but its purpose is to help the believer grow in his or her relationship with the Lord.

Discover the Meaning

Christ directed His bride to teach His followers to obey all He commanded (Matt. 28:19-20). In response, the infant church made godly instruction a priority.

Read the following Scriptures and briefly explain how believers may have benefited from each instruction.

Acts 11:25-26 _learning how to live Christlike as a Christian_

Acts 17:11 _delving deeper into the truths of Scripture_

Acts 18:24-28 _helping other believers to speak + instruct others accurately_

Like worship, the ornament of godly instruction is essential to the church's transformation. Paul and Barnabas devoted a year to the instruction of new believers in Antioch. We know this intense time of discipleship had visible results because the believers in Antioch were the first to be called Christians—a name that identified them as Christ-like. The instruction Apollos received proved vital preparation for his ministry, effectively enabling him to instruct others.

> To learn more about the importance of applying God's Word to all areas of our lives, see Matthew 5:19; Colossians 3:16; and James 1:22-25.

How God Provides Instruction

We've learned what instruction is and have seen examples of how it benefited the early church. Now let's consider how God works to provide needed instruction.

1. Instruction comes from God.

Isaiah 28:26 says God teaches and instructs. What does Psalm 25:4-14 say about the character of God?

God of my Salvation, He is Compassionate w/ lovingkindness + goodness, instructs sinners in the way, leads the humble in justice, teaches the humble

What do these verses in Psalm 25 say is required to receive instruction from God? (Check all that apply.)

- ● humility
- ○ salvation
- ○ basic Bible knowledge
- ● fear (respect) of the Lord

What benefits does the psalm suggest come to the person who learns of God?

Salvation, know truth, keep His covenant, soul abide in prosperity, pardons iniquity

> HIS GOD
> INSTRUCTS
> HIM AND
> TEACHES HIM
> THE RIGHT
> WAY.
>
> ISAIAH 28:26

Godly instruction begins with God. He desires for us to learn from Him, and He instructs those who are ready and willing to listen. When we show God honor and respect, He graciously instructs us through His Holy Spirit and through His Word.

2. God equips us to instruct one another.

In Romans 15:14 Paul said he was, "convinced, my brothers, that you yourselves are full of goodness, complete in knowledge and competent to instruct one another."

Paul understood that God empowers us to instruct one another through the power of His Holy Spirit, our Counselor (John 14:26). In his final letter to Timothy, Paul emphasized the importance of equipping teachers to provide godly instruction within the church (2 Tim. 2:2). We're admonished to entrust mature believers with sound teaching so they may gently and patiently teach others.

3. God's Word is the basis for all godly instruction.

According to Romans 15:4, why was the Scripture written?

for our instruction so that through perserverance + the encouragement of the Scriptures we might have hope.

Godly instruction comes from God's written Word and "is useful for teaching, rebuking, correcting and training in righteousness" (2 Tim. 3:16). Christ's bride is to continually consult her priceless _ketubah_. The principles and wisdom within it apply to every challenge she faces. The pages of Scripture contain all the instructions she needs—the instructions you and I need—to fully prepare for Christ's return.

Discover the Meaning

Beloved, we are blessed by the early church's fervent commitment to godly instruction. Acts 5:42 reveals that "Day after day, in the temple courts and from house to house, they never stopped teaching and proclaiming the good news that Jesus is the Christ." The disciples' determination to teach new Christians what Scripture says of Christ strengthened the infant church, promoted the growth of the church body, and built up the church in love. Their Spirit-led work had far-reaching benefits for the bride and illustrated the importance of instruction within today's church.

Why did Paul proclaim Christ, admonish, and teach (Col. 1:28-29)?
○ to reach the whole world for Christ
● to present everyone perfect in Christ   _Complete in Christ_
○ to build up the body of Christ
○ to combat false teaching about Christ

Receiving instruction is not always easy or fun, but it is always for our good. Through our obedience to His instruction, God "produces a harvest of righteousness and peace," allowing us to "share in his holiness" (Heb. 12:10-11). Remember that remaining set apart and holy is an important goal of this time of preparation. The maturity produced by godly instruction also equips the church to stand firm against

to fully prepare for Christ's return
to claim the good news that Jesus is the Christ

distressing waves of difficult circumstances and destructive winds of false teaching—both of which can distract from the church's preparation for Christ's return.

Make It Personal

A recent article in *On Mission* magazine suggests the priceless ornament of instruction is being neglected in many churches today: "A new nationwide survey conducted by the Barna Research Group indicates that a large share of the people who attend Protestant or Catholic churches have adopted beliefs that conflict with the teachings of the Bible and their church."[6] The bride of Christ must return to sound biblical teaching, fulfilling her beloved's commands and preparing for His return.

Rate how seriously your church takes her responsibility to instruct Christians in godly things.

very seriously   somewhat seriously   not at all seriously

Check the statement that best reflects your personal commitment to the instruction provided through your church.
- ○ I participate if it's convenient and I have nothing else to do.
- ○ I do not feel I need further instruction; therefore, I don't participate.
- ◉ I'm anxious to receive further instruction and make it a priority.
- ○ I desire further instruction but little is offered at my church.
- ○ I'm not sure what opportunities for instruction my church provides.

Commit to learning all you can about God's plan for Christ's bride. Seek His instruction and guidance—they are precious gifts! Don't keep His Word to yourself, but share it and discuss it with your fellow Christians. Remember, you are a part of your church, and the church is charged with the responsibility of discipling believers in preparation for Christ's return. Get spiritually educated so you can share your knowledge with others. I promise—you'll be blessed by what you learn!

Day Four
Adorning Through Fellowship

When Roger and I became engaged, he gave me a beautiful diamond ring. I was fascinated by the way the stone reflected light. A friend explained that the stone sparkles as light reflects off the diamond's many polished surfaces. Together these surfaces, called facets, produce a brilliant light display. The ornaments of grace available to the church are also multifaceted. Together they reflect the stunning light of God's glory.

Today we focus on godly fellowship: the third ornament of grace available to Christ's bride. More than simple social gatherings and pot-luck dinners, fellowship is what makes the church, well … the church.

A FELLOWSHIP OF BELIEVERS

Biblical Background

According to Acts 2:42, the early believers devoted themselves to the apostles' teaching, to the breaking of bread, to prayer, and to …
- ◉ fellowship   ○ being good   ○ collecting money for the poor

The original Greek word translated "fellowship" in Acts 2:42 is *koinania*, which means "fellowship, association, community, communion, joint participation."[7] *Koinania* describes the intimate bond of community among believers—a bond that involves mutual sharing and builds a feeling of kinship within the body of Christ. The Book of Acts illustrates this relationship well.

Read Acts 2:46-47. Based on this passage, which of the following best summarizes the concept of fellowship?
- ○ eating, enjoying, and complimenting one another's cooking
- ◉ spending time with, caring for, and sharing with one another
- ○ enduring and trying to be thankful for one another

To discover more about the relationship between prayer and instruction, see Ephesians 1:17-18 and Colossians 1:9-12

Remember that the church is the fellowship of believers. Likewise, the fellowship of believers is the church. As fellow members of the bride, we are to spend time together, encouraging one another and sharing our blessings. Since this special bond helps define the church body and helps to explain how God wants us to interact with other believers, it's important that we understand its origin.

Search the Scripture

Read 1 Corinthians 1:9. Who initiated fellowship with us?

God

With whom did He call us into fellowship?

His Son, Jesus Christ our Lord

True fellowship begins with God, who called us into fellowship with Christ. As we walk in God's ways, we share in an intimate relationship with Him that allows us to fellowship with other believers. In fact, fellowship with God is required for fellowship with others (see 1 John 1:3-7). It is like divine glue binding us to God and to one another. The Apostle Paul understood this well.

Why did Paul long to see those in the church in Rome (Rom. 1:11-12)?

to share his spiritual gifts w/ other believers
that he + they would be encouraged in their faith while among them) fellowship
sharing time w/ them

Paul treasured the blessings of the fellowship of believers, and he yearned for the times of togetherness—face-to-face sharing. Because of the nature of his calling, Paul spent much of his ministry traveling. As a result, he frequently communicated through letters passed among the churches. Paul "longed" to *be with* the church in Rome so he could share his spiritual gifts and experience the special blessing of godly fellowship. Through such interaction, both Paul and the church would be mutually encouraged in their faith.

A closer look at the language in this passage reveals how essential fellowship is to the church. *Symparakaleo,* the word for *mutually encouraged* in verse 12, combines three Greek words: *syn, para,* and *kaleo. Syn* denotes "community and participation."[8] From this word we get the term *synagogue. Para* means "among, along side."[9] *Kaleo* means "to call, invite, summons."[10] This root word is also used in *ekklesia,* the Greek word for *church.* By applying these definitions to our understanding of Romans 1:11-12, we find that Paul couldn't wait to share mutual encouragement with the believers of Rome—to come alongside and be church with them.

> **Read Acts 4:32-35. Choose the answer that best completes the following. True fellowship always involves ...**
> ○ eating   ○ laughing   ◉ sharing

Acts 4:32-35 provides a beautiful illustration of godly fellowship in action. "No one claimed that any of his possessions was his own." As a result, "they shared everything they had" (v. 32). True fellowship always involves sharing.

We often use the term "church family" because it conveys an understanding of the kinship we share as Christ's followers. Paul often extended warm greetings to and among the church family, underscoring the special bond among believers (see Rom. 16:3-16; 1 Cor. 16:19-20). This extraordinary relationship is based on the fact that in Christ we are "one in heart and mind" (Acts 4:32), again reminding us that we can only experience true fellowship with other believers through the Lord.

HINDRANCES TO FELLOWSHIP

Because fellowship requires sharing, claims of ownership destroy true fellowship. Only in giving up ownership are believers free to experience genuine koinaia. However, the sharing necessary for godly fellowship is foreign to our human nature. That's why God is essential to genuine fellowship among believers.

> **List things for which believers may claim ownership within the church.**

Discover the importance of prayer to the fellowship of believers by reviewing James 5:13-16 and Paul's prayers for believers recorded in Philippians 1:8-11 and 1 Thessalonians 3:11-13.

I wish I could see your list! We take ownership of things in church in many ways. I thought of position, power, property, and the past. We take ownership of position when we say, "I've always taught that class or chaired that committee." We take ownership of power when we say, "But I always pick the theme for the spring luncheon!" Sometimes we even take ownership of church property, with selfish statements as, "This is my pew; I always sit here" or "We never loan our unused Bible study kits." At times we claim ownership of the past to control the future, insisting "we've always done it this way" or "we just don't do that here."

Beware, dear friend, selfishness—however innocent it may seem—can inflict serious damage on the bride's priceless ornament of fellowship as well as on the bride.

We sometimes forget that we are stewards—not owners—of the church. A steward owns nothing. As stewards of Christ's church, we will be required to give an account of our stewardship when He returns (see Luke 16:1-2).

> **Stop and pray that God will reveal areas in your life where you are claiming ownership of things He would have you share. Ask Him to help you. I encourage you to give up whatever He requests. It belongs to Him anyway, and you will gain much more by obediently trusting Him.**

Make It Personal

Consider the adjectives below. Underline the one from each pair that most appropriately describes the quality of fellowship in your church.

Intimate/Shallow   Inclusive/Exclusive   Consistent/Inconsistent

Why do you think some believers choose not to be involved in church today?

Very private, busy, feel not needed

God does not intend for any believer to remain apart from the church, yet many Christians are not actively involved. Although many explanations are offered to excuse this lack of activity, I believe a key factor is the lack of genuine godly fellowship in some churches. Without the glue of godly fellowship, believers become disconnected, feeling unneeded and unwanted.

I've become heavily burdened for our disconnected brothers and sisters in Christ. God has helped me to see the vital responsibility those of us who remain connected have to reach out to them. To wish things were different is not enough. We must take affirmative steps to bring disconnected believers back into full fellowship. Many are waiting to hear they are missed—that their involvement matters. God desires to use us personally to touch them and lovingly draw them back into the family. I recognize this is not an easy task but one well worth the effort. We need them as much as they need us!

What are some ways a church might try to reconnect with believers who have fallen away?

For additional examples of Paul's longing for fellowship with other believers, see Philippians 1:3-8 and 1 Thessalonians 2:17-20; 3:11-13.

Consider someone in your church who has become disconnected. What is one thing you could do this week to lovingly draw her into full fellowship?

_____

Godly fellowship requires hard work and doesn't happen overnight. We must follow God's principles for fellowship—turning loose of all claims of ownership and allowing the Holy Spirit to bind our hearts and minds together. The church must take the initiative to reconnect with believers who have fallen away, diligently working to restore the blessings of fellowship to all in the household of faith. All these things can be accomplished through the power of God's Holy Spirit.

The ornament of godly fellowship enriches the church and fulfills her ultimate purpose of making God known. It also unifies believers, bringing glory to God and preparing Christ's bride for His return. The church's ability to withstand the fierce storms of this world is often related to the divine glue of godly fellowship.

As we conclude today's lesson, I can't help but think about how much I long to meet each of you! Our shared journey has sparked a unique fellowship among us. I believe "it is right for me to feel this way about all of you, since I have you in my heart … [and] all of you share in God's grace with me" (Phil. 1:7).

Day 5
Adorning Through Evangelism

I hope our look at the ornaments of grace available to Christ's bride has helped you better understand the church's responsibilities during this time on the kingdom calendar. As we've learned, getting ready for Christ's return requires that the bride actively work with God to prepare for the coming wedding celebration.

Today we'll consider one final ornament of grace: evangelism. While each ornament points to God's grace, evangelism is a dazzling reflection of the miraculous grace God bestows on those who love Him. But like instruction, evangelism is a word that can evoke a strong response.

> Getting ready for Christ's return requires that the bride actively work with God to prepare for the coming wedding celebration.

Your church may use another word—such as outreach, missions, or ministry—to describe its efforts to share Christ. What term does your church typically use to describe its efforts to win the lost?

_____

How do you feel when that word is mentioned?

_____

When we hear the word *evangelism* or one of its synonyms come up in conversation, many of us tense up. Our palms get damp and we want to change the subject. Some suggest such responses are usually the result of fear and guilt. But why do we fear evangelism? I think some people fear it because they don't understand what evangelism requires and aren't sure how to apply it to their Christian walk.

HIS WITNESSES

Biblical Background

Evangelism is a central message of the New Testament. Possibly we would feel different about the term if we consider the meaning. The word *evangelism* comes from the Greek word *euangelion*. The Greek prefix *eu* means good. The word *euangelion* is derived from *angelos*, meaning messenger. You probably could have guessed that the English word *angel* comes from this Greek word. In classical Greek the term originally designated the reward given to a messenger of victory or good tidings. The messenger's good news brought relief to the recipients; therefore he was rewarded. Later the term came to mean the good news or message itself.

How differently might you feel about evangelism if you thought of yourself as an angel bringing a message of victory, relief, and joy?

_____

_____

Search the Scriptures

Read Matthew 28:16-20. Summarize Jesus' command.

Go + teach + make disciples of all the nations

Read 1 Timothy 2:1-6. According to verse 4, what does God want?

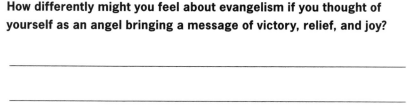

all men to be saved + to come to the knowledge of the truth + accept Jesus as His Son

God desires that all be saved. He wants everyone to enter into a personal relationship with Him, accepting Jesus as His Son, asking Him to forgive their sins, allowing Him to transform their lives. John 3:16 reminds us that "God so loved the world that he gave his one and only Son, that whoever believes in him shall not perish but have eternal life." Scripture is clear that God desires all be saved, but how can they accept Christ when they have not heard His story? Evangelism provides an answer to that dilemma. Simply stated, evangelism is sharing the truth of Christ with those who do not know Him. Any action to communicate the truth and love of Christ falls under the category of evangelism.

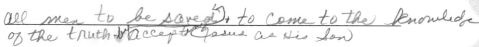

EVANGELISM

IS SHARING THE

TRUTH

OF CHRIST

WITH THOSE WHO

DO NOT KNOW HIM.

Discover the Meaning

Last year we felt God calling our family to host Joyce, a foreign exchange student from Taiwan. I had no doubt God's primary objective in placing her in our hands was to share the love of Christ with her. Since Joyce's father is Buddhist and she lists her own religion as Taoism, this could have been her only opportunity to hear the gospel. What I didn't realize was God planned to do a mighty work in my own heart through this beautiful young woman.

I didn't want to attack Joyce with Scripture. Righteously insisting that our "Western" religion was better than her family's Eastern one would not do. So I made it my goal to witness to her by showing and sharing—by showing her the love of Christ in everyday life and then by sharing what Christ has done for me as the Spirit provided opportunities. Happily, our entire church family joined in the effort to witness to Joyce and to pray for her salvation. She still talks about how much she loved going to church with our family.

Tragically, I fear many churches and individuals have lost the urgency of the command to share Christ. Even as I write that sentence, I am burdened by its reality. It represents a serious matter because the bride of Christ will not be prepared for her beloved's return if she does not urgently and diligently evangelize.

How can we conquer our fear at the thought of evangelizing? First, we must understand the ornament of evangelism as a wonderful blessing. It offers us opportunity to share who God is and what He has done for us. God does not ask us to evangelize on our own power. He gave us a helper.

Rewrite Acts 1:8 in your own words. *Share the message of salvation*

When the Holy Spirit enters my life, I will receive the His power + be able to witness — Go, tell, + pray for those who have not received salvation

As we've learned, the mission Christ gave the church is accomplished through a divine partnership. While that mission requires that Christ's bride share the message of salvation with the world, the church is not expected to save anyone. Only God can do that. Let's pause and let that one sink in. This simple truth has relieved my greatest fears about evangelism. We do not save anyone—God does. We are not responsible for the response of those with whom we share. That is between them and God. Individual believers and the church are to go, tell, and pray for those who have not received salvation.

Our precious Joyce has returned to Taiwan. We lovingly and urgently shared the message of salvation through Christ alone. Sadly, she has yet to receive Christ as her personal Savior. We continue to stay in contact with her, to share what God is doing in our lives, and to pray for her salvation. The outcome remains in God's hands, but my family and our church family are blessed in knowing we did what we are called to do.

Through the power and under the control of the Spirit, the church can be an active witness for Christ. Christ's bride can tell the world who Jesus is, spreading His message of mercy throughout the world and explaining how others can find salvation through Him.

FELLOW EVANGELISTS

Search the Scripture

How do we know that the early church was active in evangelism?

_____

The fact that the church is still alive and thriving testifies to the faithful evangelistic outreach of Christ's earliest followers. These bold men and women spread the gospel throughout the ancient world, and the Bible's record of their actions gives us some principles of evangelism that still apply today.

1. *They lived what Jesus taught*.
Only a disciple can lead others to follow Him. By following Jesus' example of loving others, living godly lives, and giving to those in need, the early Christians radiated God's love. Through the power of the Holy Spirit, that radiance drew others to Jesus.

2. *They arrayed the church in ornaments of grace*.
Look for evidence of each of the four ornaments of grace: worship, instruction, fellowship, and evangelism in Matthew 28:16-20. Note your findings in the margin.

In verse 17 the disciples worshiped Jesus; they spontaneously responded to a personal encounter with the living God! The other three ornaments appear in Jesus' command to His bride. "Make disciples" refers to salvation, which is the end goal of evangelism. "Baptizing them in the name of the Father and of the Son and of the Holy Spirit" represents the new birth into the family (fellowship) of believers. "Teaching them to obey everything I have commanded" refers to godly instruction. Throughout the New Testament, we find evidence that the disciples regularly put Jesus' instructions into action (see Acts 2:42-47; 4:8-13).

Make It Personal

We too should strive to grow in our relationship with Christ, following both His example and His commands.

How important is evangelism to your church?

extremely important — somewhat important — not important at all

List some ways a church can share Christ with the lost.

[handwritten margin notes, left side:]
vs 17 - when they saw Him, they worshiped Him
vs 20 - teaching them
vs 19 - make disciples & baptize them
vs 20 - I am w/ you always

[handwritten notes at bottom:]
Pray for them, outreach
TV ministry - on-line newsletters & ministry, publish lesson book, mission @ home & to foreign countries, respond to disasters, invite unbelievers to church or participation in your bible study

Think of someone in your life who does not know Christ. What can you do to share His love with that person?

_____

Evangelism is an essential part of the church's preparation for Christ's return. In sharing Christ, the church makes God known (Eph. 3:10). The church can share Christ in many different ways. What is effective in my church in Northern Wyoming may be very different from what is effective in your church. What worked in your church in the past may not work today. While we may need new methods of outreach, our God remains the same. He is always faithful and always at work.

While salvation itself is the work of the Spirit, the church must make continual evangelistic efforts around the world. Part of the evangelistic task is to pray unceasingly for the lost. God calls the church to pray for those who do not know Christ. Through prayer we join with Jesus in interceding for the lost. Paul understood the priority of prayer in evangelism.

Why do you think Paul used the words "urge" and "first of all" in 1 Timothy 2:1-2?

prayers first w/ Thanksgiving + petitions before anything else.

Unfortunately, many of us approach life—and even evangelism—without first consulting God for His help and guidance. In verse 1 Paul suggested that we do the opposite and pray before doing anything else. First, we should pray for our family members who do not know Christ, thanking God for them and interceding on their behalf. We should also pray for others we know personally as well as those we don't know. We are to continually pray that others will come to know God.

How often does your church pray for the salvation of the lost?

never — rarely — often

As we continue to prepare Christ's bride for the coming heavenly wedding celebration, we must not neglect the ornament of evangelism. Through evangelism the church grows and moves toward the completion of her beloved's mission. Each new believer brings her one step closer to His long-awaited return.

What a joy it's been to examine the church's priceless ornaments of God's grace! This week's study has made me more aware of the different ways God is preparing the church for Christ's return. I hope you too have developed a greater appreciation for the church's ornaments—worship, instruction, fellowship, and evangelism. Each is a beautiful reflection of God's grace working through us to adorn Christ's bride for the coming wedding celebration.

Christ, the divine bridegroom, eagerly observes His bride's preparation of her ornaments of grace. Next week we'll hear His loving words of encouragement to her as we listen to His urgent messages to His beloved church.

Met
July 18, 2011

Joyce
Barbara
Ann

Messages from the Bridegroom

5

WHEN I FIRST MET MY HUSBAND, HE WAS A CORPORATE PILOT, OFTEN GONE DAYS AT A TIME. Even after becoming engaged we sometimes didn't see each other for weeks because of the distance and our busy schedules.

During those days of separation, Roger frequently sent me notes of encouragement (often including flowers!). "Do you miss me?" "I can't wait to see you!" "I love you!" Every time I received one of his notes I blushed with happiness and became increasingly eager for our approaching wedding. His letters of encouragement made me love him all the more.

I still cherish those faded, handwritten messages. Decades later, Roger's notes still have a powerful affect on me. Opening the aging envelopes, I discover afresh the joy of receiving a message from my beloved.

Jesus Christ, the divine bridegroom, desires to convey love messages to His bride too. Thoughtfully and with compassion He composes each priceless message to meet her needs during this time of betrothal separation. This week we examine some of these precious and compelling messages to Christ's church. Together we'll find these powerful passages reveal remarkable insight into the eternal depth of Christ's enduring love for His bride and shed a brighter light on the source of her strength for the preparations ahead.

I can hardly wait to begin!

Day One
You Are Built on a Firm Foundation

The betrothal preparations are time consuming and can be extremely challenging. The bride needs reassurance that her efforts are on track and the groom has not changed his intentions. The loving bridegroom responds to his beloved's concerns with encouragement, assuring her of his devotion and commitment.

Some may wrongly assume that Jesus sits in heaven, oblivious to the preparation and condition of His bride. Those who hold such views miss a beautiful truth: Jesus Christ is an incredibly loving and devoted bridegroom. He not only cares about His bride but He notes both her needs and her loyalty. With this in mind, know that Jesus has some important things to say to His beloved. Through the pages of Scripture He speaks to her, offering messages of love, hope, encouragement, and even correction.

I pray you'll find each message we read as personal and relevant today as when it was first delivered because when Jesus speaks, His bride—and her attendants—should stop and listen.

To discover more on how love messages were used in ancient times, see the Song of Songs in the Old Testament.

FOUR IMPORTANT MESSAGES

We begin with a look at four key messages Christ gave the church during His earthly ministry. These encouragements remind today's church of her divine identity and challenge her to remain firmly rooted in Jesus.

Search the Scripture

Read Matthew 16:13-19. What does this passage suggest about the church? (Check all that apply.)

- ◉ The church belongs to Christ.
- ○ The church is not safe.
- ◉ The church is founded on who Jesus is.
- ○ Peter is the head of the church.
- ◉ The church has been given authority and power.
- ◉ Christ has made the church secure.

Christ is the head of His church
— Keys to the kingdom
The church will be given according to God's
divine timetable

Discover the Meaning

One of the things that makes Christ's relationship with His bride unique is that He created her. The church was formed in the womb of Jesus' earthly ministry, and the Spirit breathed life into her at Pentecost. Her formation provides valuable insight into how Jesus views His bride, thus providing the background we'll need to better understand His messages to her. Let's consider the significance of each of Jesus' four messages regarding the church as we delve more deeply into the Matthew passage. In the previous exercise I checked all but the second and fifth responses.

1. The church belongs to Christ; she exists at the will of God.

According to Matthew 16:13-19, who is building the church?

Jesus

Jesus' "I will" declaration reflects the divine origin of His bride: She exists as a result of Christ's work and influence. "Will" provides a wordplay in English: The church exists at God's will—not man's. This fact may seem elementary, but it has revolutionized my life.

For many years I saw the church as a building—a place where Christians go to get closer to God. I neglected to recognize the church as a living part of divine creation. This misconception affected my attitudes and actions toward the church. I saw my involvement as voluntary and my choice to participate a reflection of my own goodness. When I recognized the significance of the fact that the church exists at God's will instead of man's, my approach to church began to change.

What difference does it make to you that the church exists at God's will?

Beloved, the fact that the church exists by divine choice proves that her purpose and continued existence are guaranteed by God and are not dependent on the will of man. The church has received a divine charter that will never be revoked. Praise God, no matter how attacked the church becomes, she will stand. Why? Her future is securely in the hands of her groom, again reminding us that the church's future does not depend on our work but on God's power. What a blessing to attend the bride of Christ, knowing that the outcome is fully guaranteed!

According to Matthew 16:18, who "owns" the church?
○ Peter   ○ the members   ◉ Jesus   ○ the established religious leaders

Did you notice that Jesus used the possessive pronoun "My" to refer to His bride? The church belongs to Him. He is committed to building her up. The Greek word for *build* is *oikodomeo* and means "to build up, edify, strengthen."[1] Christ's reference to "building" His church points to the church's process of becoming the fully prepared bride. Through the Holy Spirit Christ edifies and strengthens His beloved, preparing her for eternal glory. What joy and reassurance those words bring!

2. The church is founded on the truth of who Jesus is.

According to Matthew 16:18, on what would Christ build His church?
○ a high mountain   ◉ a rock   ○ the gates of Hades

Match the Scripture references with the foundation statements.

_C_ Isaiah 28:16

_A_ Matthew 21:42

_B_ 1 Corinthians 3:11

a. The stone the builders rejected became the capstone.

b. Jesus is the foundation already laid.

c. God laid a precious cornerstone for a sure foundation.

According to Isaiah 28:16, on what "rock" is the church built?

○ a granite stone   ○ Peter   ○ the disciples   ● Jesus Christ

Isaiah 28:16 points to Christ as a precious cornerstone. Without question, the church is built on the rock of Jesus Christ, our firm and lasting foundation.

When Peter became a disciple, Jesus gave him the name *Peter* (*petros*) meaning *stone* (John 1:42). Regrettably, some are confused by the language of Matthew 16:18, mistakenly naming Peter as the church's cornerstone. Fortunately, the original Greek words make Jesus' meaning more clear. "You are *petros* (a stone) and on this *petra* (large rock) I will build my church."[2] In Matthew 16 Jesus used a play on words to help Peter and the others make an important distinction. In essence He said, *I will not build my church on who you are, but on who I am*. In other words, the church is not built on man's works but through God's power.

How did Peter understand Jesus words according to 1 Peter 2:4-6?

Christ is the solid rock - the cornerstone. The Christ of our destiny.

Peter understood that Christ, God's only Son, is the cornerstone on which the church is built. Unfortunately, not everyone shares his understanding. Some believe Jesus was a good man with some good ideas. Others think He was a great prophet who is now dead. Still others feel Jesus is a legendary figure.

Different opinions of Jesus will always exist—some accurate and others not. Such perceptions are why it's so important that we base our belief about Jesus on Scripture. We must not lose sight of an important point Christ makes in asking His disciples who others say He is: The church is built on the truth of His identity—the Son of the living God—not on the world's opinion of Him.

Compare Luke 12:51 and John 10:19-21. Then mark each of the following statements true (T) or false (F).

_T_ Until Jesus returns, people will always be divided about who He is.

_F_ Jesus didn't know people would disagree about Him.

_T_ The opinions of man do not change the truth of who Jesus is.

How might the world's opinions about Jesus affect the church's understanding of who He is?

_____

_____

Hymn
On Christ, the solid rock, I stand. All other ground is sinking sand.

God's only Son on which the church is built

3. The church has been given spiritual power and divine authority.

Jesus established His church and promised to give her "the keys of the kingdom of heaven" (Matthew 16:19). The keys include spiritual power and divine authority. Notice Jesus said, "I will give" not "I am giving" in verse 19, signifying that the power and authority would be given according to God's divine timetable.

Before we consider the meaning behind Jesus' description of the nature of the church's power and authority, let's take a look at the only other time during His earthly ministry that Jesus spoke specifically of His church.

Compare Matthew 18:15-20 with Matthew 16:19. What similarities do you find in Jesus' words?

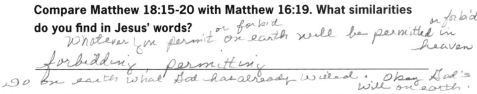

Whatever you permit or forbid on earth will be permitted or forbid in heaven
forbidding, permitting
Do on earth what God has already willed. Obey God's will on earth.

Almost as if to elaborate on the promise given in Matthew 16:19, Jesus added: "'Whatever you bind on earth will be bound in heaven, and whatever you loose on earth will be loosed in heaven'" (Matt. 18:18). Though Jesus' reference to "binding and loosing" seems strange to us, these terms were familiar to the disciples. Religious teachers often used this phrase to refer to forbidding or permitting.

The Expanded Translation offers the following explanation: "'And whatever you bind on earth [forbid to be done], shall have been already bound ... in heaven; and whatever you loose on earth [permit to be done], shall have already been loosed in heaven.'" Jesus did not say that God would obey what they did on earth, but that they should do on earth what God had already willed. The church does not get man's will done in heaven; it obeys God's will on earth."[3]

How does Acts 2:33 demonstrate the fulfillment of Jesus' promise to give His bride power and authority?
- ○ It assures us that Jesus will return.
- ○ It gives instructions for forming a new government.
- ● It affirms that Jesus poured out the Spirit on believers.

4. Christ has made the church secure; she is assured of victory.

What do you think Jesus meant by "the gates of Hades will not overcome it" in Matthew 16:18?

The Church will prevail

"Gates of Hades" represents the organized power of evil that fights against the church by opposing the gospel and persecuting believers.[4] Throughout history, the church's enemies have fought to destroy her. They still do. But Jesus promised to preserve and secure His beloved bride. His words are not a promise of freedom from difficulties but an assurance of the final outcome. Though the church and individual believers face hardships, they will prevail.

"THE CHURCH
DOES NOT GET
MAN'S WILL DONE
IN HEAVEN;
IT OBEYS
GOD'S WILL
ON EARTH."

How might Christians experience hardship (see 2 Cor. 4:7-9)?

afflicted in every way, but not crushed; perplexed but not despairing. Persecuted, struck down

How does this passage support the promise that the bride and her faithful attendants will prevail through hardships?

The surpassing greatness of the power will be of God and not from ourselves. persecuted but not forsaken, struck down but not destroyed

Make It Personal

Today's lesson includes four important messages from Jesus to His beloved bride. List them, and circle the one you find most moving.

The Church belongs to Christ & exists @ the will of God

The church is founded on who Jesus is

The church has been given spiritual power and divine authority

Christ has made the Church Secure assurance of victory

What do you think God is saying to you personally through the message you circled?

great hope

How can your church remain grounded in the truth of Jesus Christ?

How can your church respond to her enemies with an attitude of victory?

Today opposition to the truth of God's Word continues to grow. In many parts of the world, persecution is on the rise. Even in America, a nation founded on Christian principles, the church is often openly ridiculed.

But Jesus left His bride with four important messages to cling to in the midst of history's storms, establishing Himself as her firm foundation. He secured her future and granted her all power and authority needed to faithfully prepare for His return. His message is worth repeating!

Day Two
Keep Me First

Scripture is so precious! In it we find the marriage contract between Christ and His bride. We see promises, encouragements, and even loving rebuke. While each book adds unique threads to the tapestry of divine relationship, Revelation offers Christ's clearest expectations for His bride. Today we return to Revelation to examine urgent mid-betrothal messages from Jesus to the church. You may have previously studied Jesus' seven messages to His bride, but I hope that all we've learned has prepared us to see the divine bridegroom's intimate words in a fresh light.

The Book of Revelation has been the subject of much debate. Godly scholars sometimes disagree on the interpretation of its symbolism and the order of events described. However, Christ's call to readiness is not dependent on any one interpretation of end time events. Christ will return for His bride, and she must be ready.

Search the Scripture

To whom was the Revelation originally given (Rev. 1:4,11) and for whom was it written (Rev. 22:16)?

given to _the 7 Churches in Asia_ **written for** _the Churches_

Through John's Revelation, Jesus clearly demonstrated a passionate desire to communicate with His bride. As we read His messages to the early church, we can almost hear the urgency in His voice. I believe those communications become increasingly urgent as the betrothal progresses.

Read Revelation 1. What do the gold lampstands symbolize (v. 20)?

○ angels ● the churches ○ the message of the gospel

Many of the symbols used in Revelation relate back to the Hebrew Scriptures. The lampstand image used to represent the church is from the Old Testament. But since most of us aren't familiar with ancient lampstands, we'll need to do some digging.

Read Exodus 25:31-40 which describes the lampstand God commanded Moses to have made for the tabernacle.

The lampstand described in Exodus 25 had a single shaft with three branches extending from each side for a total of seven lampholders. According to verse 37, seven cups or "lamps" are on one lampstand.

Now turn back to Revelation 1:12. How many lampstands did John see?

Seven

Read Matthew 25:1-3. What did the wedding attendants carry to meet the bridegroom?

lamps

Which of the following does Matthew 5:14-16 not tell us?

○ Individual believers are the light of the world.

○ We should put our lamps on a lampstand.

○ When our lights are on the lampstand, they become more visible.

◉ We should keep our lamps hidden in our homes.

Discover the Meaning

We know that in Revelation each lampstand represents the church. What might the individual lamps on the lampholders represent?

○ the church building　◉ individual believers　○ persecution

Revelation doesn't reveal what the lamps themselves represent, but Jesus used the lamp as an illustration of the individual believer. By telling believers to put their lamps on a lampstand—an image clearly used in Revelation to represent the church—Jesus confirmed the importance of each believer's local church involvement (Matt. 5:14-16). Later, in Matthew 25, Jesus again used a lamp to illustrate the believer's role in attending His bride. I believe the lampstands in Revelation 1 further illustrate the vital connection between believers and the bride.

What is the significance of Jesus' physical location in Revelation 1:13?

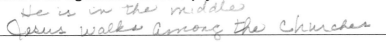

He is in the middle
Jesus walks among the churches

The same messages Jesus revealed to John regarding the early churches still apply to us. Even today the bridegroom walks among the churches, inspecting His bride and evaluating her readiness. As we consider each of Christ's messages, think about your own church. Continually ask yourself, "How does my church measure up to Christ's standards?"

Because we'll focus on the substance of Jesus' messages, I've grouped them by related subject rather than the order they appear in Scripture. Let's begin with Jesus' messages regarding priorities, directed to the churches in Ephesus and Smyrna.

MESSAGE TO THE CHURCH AT EPHESUS

Search the Scripture

Filled with pagan idolatry and dominated by the worship of Diana, the goddess of fertility, Ephesus was a rich seaport city located in what is now Southwest Turkey. The church in Ephesus enjoyed great leadership under Paul's guidance. Paul planted this church and spent more time with her than any other. Timothy and John helped to care for her. Early tradition holds that John the apostle later pastored this church. But perhaps the Ephesus church relied too much on their human leadership—slowly losing sight of the fact that Jesus Himself was in control.

Carefully read Revelation 2:1-7. How did Jesus identify Himself?

○ the One who has the sharp, double-edged sword

● the One who holds the seven stars and walks among the lampstands

○ the Amen, the faithful and true witness

What encouragement did Jesus offer the church in Ephesus (vv. 2-3)?

that they toiled & endured + perservered + do not tolerate evil men

What specific fault did Jesus find in them (v. 4)?

left your first love

What did Jesus instruct them to do (v. 5)?

Repent + do the deeds you first did

If they ignored His warning, what would Jesus do to them (v. 5)?

Jesus would remove your lampstand out of its place (The church would die out)

The following are signs that a local church may be simply "doing" church rather than actively longing for the bridegroom's return.

- General contentment to sit and soak with no interest in serving and sowing.
- General motivation comes through guilt and shame rather than hope and joy.
- General focus on keeping things the way they have always been instead of pressing ahead to go somewhere new with God.

Discover the Meaning

Jesus began His message with loving words of encouragement. He commended her and recognized her hard work. Yet while the Ephesian church did many good things for Christ, she was still forsaking Him. This warning illustrates that a church can labor for Christ and even endure hardships in His name, yet neglect to continually acknowledge His rightful place as her loving bridegroom.

Preparing for a wedding is rarely easy. Dresses and flowers must be ordered. Music selected. Dates set. Invitations addressed. Yet in the midst of the chaos, the bride must remember that her work should revolve around the groom. She can't neglect the reason for her preparations—her beloved husband-to-be.

Love for her bridegroom should motivate the bride's actions during the betrothal. The bride's faith in Christ and her hope in His return produce fruitful work and inspire true endurance. Jesus, ever faithful and attentive, instructed the church to repent of the sin of forsaking Him and to return to Him by doing what she did at the first: working with focus and in anticipation of His soon return. Christ called His bride to renew her commitment to Him.

Make It Personal

What motivates your church to do good things? Does Christ still have first place in her heart, or does she allow the desire to be successful or to compete with other churches guide her actions?

With your answer in mind, how would you rate your church's love relationship with Christ?

She has forsaken her first love. — Sometimes she's in love and other times not. — She is experiencing an exciting, growing romance.

How can a church guard against doing right things for wrong reasons?

_____

Do you recall a time when you did the right thing for the wrong reason? ○ yes ○ no **What are some ways to test your motives for serving to make sure they are pure?**

_____

_____

MESSAGE TO THE CHURCH AT SARDIS

Located about 50 miles east of Ephesus, the once wealthy city of Sardis was also a center for trade. But Sardis, dominated by wickedness, fell into decline. At the time of the Revelation, the Sardis church lived in denial–living in her past splendor while ignoring her deterioration.

Search the Scripture

Read Revelation 3:1-6. How did Jesus identify Himself in this passage?
   ○ as the One who is the First and the Last
   ◉ as the One who holds the seven spirits of God
   ○ as the One who has the sharp, double-edged sword

Jesus offered little encouragement for the Sardis church. However, He did offer hope. What good news did He share in verses 4 and 5?

He would not erase the name of the ones who overcome (the few believers left) who remained faithful would be rewarded) *from the book of life* & will confess *his name before His Father & before His angels.*

What warning did Jesus give in verse 3?

Wake-up

The Sardis church had a "reputation of being alive" (v. 1). She was very busy and from outward appearances probably looked healthy. Yet the truth was that the church had become more of a reflection of her surroundings than of God's glory.

Jesus mentioned neither doctrinal problems nor persecution in Sardis. This suggests complacency as a primary factor in her decline. Relying on past deeds and reputation while ignoring her spiritual decline, she became totally ineffective. But Jesus didn't cast the wayward church aside as hopeless. He reminded her that she had what she needed to be complete (see 2 Pet. 1:3-4). He also encouraged her that a few believers at Sardis remained faithful and would be rewarded (v. 4).

Discover the Meaning

Though Jesus acknowledged that some in the church had not soiled their garments, it seems that the overall activities of the Sardis church were having little or no spiritual effect. They had discarded the inward preparations of her beautiful ornaments of grace—worship, instruction, fellowship, and evangelism—for the sake of *appearing* active. Perhaps the bride at Sardis became so caught up in doing church that she ceased to long for her bridegroom's return.

> **Have you ever tried to appear busier than you really were?** ○ yes ○ no
> **Why do you think we sometimes emphasize appearance over reality?**
> - ○ fear of what people think
> - ○ desire to gain approval
> - ○ habit
> - ○ lack of personal security
> - ○ works-based identity
> - ○ other _____

Jesus implored His bride to wake up! Some churches become so comfortable that they fall asleep! It's time we as attendants of the bride take careful inventory of what we're doing and why. We must rediscover what's most important to the divine bridegroom, exchanging unproductive religious activity for actions that are wholly focused on pleasing Him, actions that truly prepare for His return.

Make It Personal

> **Which of your church's activities best prepare for Christ's return?**
>
> _____
>
> **In what ways are you involved in the activities listed above?**
>
> _____
>
> **How often does your church talk about Christ's return?**
>
> rarely — seldom — occasionally — frequently
>
> **Do you long for the return of Christ?** ● yes ○ no
> **If so, how do others know how important His return is to you?**
>
> _____

The churches at Ephesus and Sardis did many of the right things for the wrong reasons. Both were in danger of dying because they had disconnected themselves from Christ, the source of life. Ephesus had forsaken her first love. Sardis had forsaken her responsibilities to prepare for her bridegroom's return. The bride of Christ and her attendants must make preparation for His return our first priority. Simply "doing" church is not an option.

Day Three
Do Not Be Afraid *persecution*

As I begin to consider fear, my thoughts immediately fly to my son. Years ago, several weeks before school began, Taylor started saying, "I'm not going to kindergarten!" And it wasn't that he thought he had a choice in the matter; he was simply afraid.

Over the centuries the church has also wrestled fears. The fear of persecution. The fear of suffering. The fear of ineffectiveness. The fear of weakness. Today we examine Jesus' messages for two churches facing these great difficulties, and we'll find He understood what they went through. We'll hear His compassion as He lovingly reminded His bride of the call to faithfulness, assuring her that she can conquer her fears by steadfastly placing her hope in Him.

MESSAGE TO THE CHURCH AT SMYRNA

Smyrna was the site of one early church well acquainted with fear. A port city located about five miles north of Ephesus, it is now called, Izmir, Turkey. This prosperous seaport was named after its primary commercial product, myrrh.[5]

Search the Scripture

> **Read Revelation 2:8-11. How did Jesus identify Himself in verse 8?**
> ○ as the Son of God whose eyes are like fire and feet like bronze
> ○ as the Amen, the faithful and true witness
> ◉ as the First and the Last, who died and came to life again

> **How did Jesus encourage the Smyrna church in verses 9-10?**

Be faithful until death and I will give you the crown of life

> **What warning did Jesus give the believers in Smyrna (v. 10)?**

Do not fear what you are about to suffer you will have tribulation

For further reading about the "second death" that Jesus referred to in Revelation 2:11, see Revelation 20:14-15; 21:1-8.

The church at Smyrna experienced twofold persecution for her faith. First, Smyrna was a center of the Roman imperial cult and anyone refusing to say, "Caesar is Lord" would be severely punished. According to church history, the pastor of the Smyrna church was burned at the stake.[6] The second source of attack came from Smyrna's Jewish population, some of whom apparently openly ridiculed the church and slandered her reputation. The Smyrna church may have never gained the approval of men, but she received the praise of her bridegroom (Rev. 2:9).

Read 2 Timothy 3:12. According to this passage, those who live a godly life in Christ will be …

○ admired   ○ happy   ◉ persecuted   ○ sorry

What does Acts 14:21-23 reveal about entering the kingdom of God?

you must remain faithful through your trials + tribulation By continuing in the faith for through many tribulations we must enter the kingdom of God

As these passages illustrate, the church of Smyrna was not alone in facing persecution; other churches endured similar threats. To all churches who suffer for Him, Jesus identifies Himself as the conqueror of death. He assures His distressed bride that suffering and physical death are not final. By remaining faithful to Him, the persecuted church will find victory: "Be faithful even to the point of death," Jesus admonished them, "and I will give you the crown of life" (Rev. 20:10).

How do hardships endured for the sake of Christ benefit the church (2 Cor. 4:16–5:1)? (Place a star beside the correct answers.)

the quick passage of time   ✓ daily renewal
✓ eternal glory   fame and recognition
✓ heaven as an eternal home   dignity and respect

What should a church suffering persecution do (2 Cor. 4:18)?
◉ Fix her eyes on the eternal.
○ Fight back against the persecutors.
○ Ask God to remove the persecution.

Don't miss the tenderness of Jesus' words, "I know your afflictions … I know the slander" (Rev. 2:9). Jesus comforts His bride with the knowledge that He truly understands. Christ is no stranger to persecution–even to death (see Isa. 53:3-4,7). Yet even after He'd been wrongly accused, mocked, slandered, beaten, flogged, and nailed to a cross–Jesus remained centered on the divine plan. Though others might have hurled insults and curses at soldiers who so methodically abused them, Jesus found compassion for His tormentors: "Father, forgive them, for they do not know what they are doing" (Luke 23:34). What an encouragement to know Jesus sees every affliction of His bride and understands what she is going through!

What does Hebrews 12:1-3 tell believers to consider "so that [they] will not grow weary and lose heart"?

Fix our eyes on Jesus + Consider Him who has endured such hostility by sinners against Him

Discover the Meaning

Having experienced great suffering and even death Himself, Jesus offered valuable instruction to His bride: "Do not be afraid" (Rev. 2:10). Let's consider examples of how Jesus encouraged others who were afraid.

Which of the following best completes Jesus' words to the synagogue leader in Mark 5:36 "Don't be afraid; just ... "

○ pray ○ be happy ● believe

Acts 18:9-10 describes a vision in which Jesus encouraged Paul. Paraphrase Jesus' words to him.

Trust Me & do not fear
Speak freely w/o fear for I am w/you.

Surrounded by an increasingly evil world, the church today is sometimes fearful. But Jesus reminded His bride that He can conquer anything and asked that she put her faith and trust in Him. Through unwavering focus on her bridegroom, the bride of Christ can be fearless in any circumstance.

Make It Personal

The church that lives according to God's purposes will endure persecution. Historically the persecuted or threatened church has generally thrived, showing herself to be pure, powerful, and passionate—three qualities that Christ desires she reflect. As the return of Christ approaches, the persecution will increase. The bride must stand firm in hope, trusting in her beloved's ability to protect her and His promise of a crown of life (Rev. 3:10). As insults and difficulties test the bride, she is wise to recall that Jesus recognized the church in Smyrna as spiritually rich (see Rev. 2:19). He encouraged her and gave her strength.

How has your church been attacked or persecuted for Christ?

_____

What can you do to demonstrate faith in Christ in the midst of fear?

Stand firm & put on the full armour of God
His Word of Truth.

Has Christ comforted you when you were persecuted for your beliefs?
○ yes ○ no **If so, explain.**

_____

_____

MESSAGE TO THE CHURCH AT PHILADELPHIA

To learn more about Christ's encouragement to smaller churches, read Matthew 13:31-32, 18:20; Luke 12:32.

Sometimes fear within the church is not linked so much to trials or persecutions as to weakness. Such was the case in the church of Philadelphia–a city located on the main route from Rome to the east. Philadelphia, because it was overrun with many temples, was sometimes called "Little Athens."[7]

Search the Scripture

Read Revelation 3:7-13. How did Jesus identify Himself in verse 7?
- ○ as the First and the Last
- ○ as the One with the sharp double-edged sword
- ● as the holy and true

Perhaps in response to the many false gods of Philadelphia's temples, Jesus reminded His bride that He alone is holy and true. He alone holds the keys to eternal life.

How does John 14:6 support Jesus' description of Himself?

No one comes to the Father but through Jesus.

What three encouragements did Jesus offer the church of Philadelphia (Rev. 3: 9-11)?

I will keep you from the hour of Testing because you kept My word. I am coming quickly; hold fast Be faithful + no one will take your crown

Don't overlook Jesus' encouragement to the church at Philadelphia in her continued faithfulness to His word and His name. He was pleased and aware that in spite of her frailty, she kept the command to endure (v. 10).

How can our weakness become strength (2 Cor. 12:9)?

By allowing The power of Christ to dwell in us in the midst of our weakness

IT'S NOT THE SIZE OF A CHURCH THAT DETERMINES HER EFFECTIVENESS; IT'S HER FAITH IN THE BRIDEGROOM'S ABILITY TO PROVIDE.

The Philadelphia church was neither large nor strong. Her limitations were likely due to her size, lack of resources, and perhaps the fact that the church was surrounded by pagan temples. Yet Jesus did not discount her. In fact, He made special provisions for her, obviously more impressed with her faithfulness than He was concerned by her "limited strength."

We sometimes forget that it's not the size of a church that determines her effectiveness; it's her faith in the bridegroom's ability to provide. Christ praised the church in Philadelphia because she allowed His perfect power to shine in the midst of her weakness.

Discover the Meaning

When the world seems to pull against them from every side, struggling churches are in danger of taking their eyes off the goal. But opposition is a part of ministry. The church must not allow it to overshadow divine opportunities. In the case of the church at Philadelphia, Jesus pointed out a ministry opportunity that the church didn't see. Perhaps she didn't see it because the opposition had blinded the church to the open door before her. Whatever the reason, Jesus warned the church in Philadelphia not to miss "the open door that no one can shut" (Rev. 3:8). No one can close the doors of opportunity as long as He chooses to leave them open.

In Scripture, an open door represents a ministry opportunity. In Revelation 3 Jesus placed before the Philadelphia church a special opportunity for ministry. We can't know for certain what Jesus had in mind for that church. However, we can be sure it was important to the kingdom because Jesus did not want her to miss it!

Make It Personal

Jesus still places ministry opportunities before His bride—opportunities carefully selected for each local church, regardless of size or material wealth—ministries for which He has already equipped her.

What are some ministries in which your church is currently involved?

Laurel Creek Manor.

What ministry "open doors" does your church need not to overlook?

Has God opened a door of ministry for you? If so, explain how you responded. If not, pray and ask God to help you make sure you don't miss any doors of opportunity He opens.

When there is no more work to be done here, He will call us Home.

Both the church at Smyrna and the church at Philadelphia endured trials—hardships the bridegroom noticed. Jesus sees His bride's struggles. He knows her frailties. He understands her fear. But even in her weakness, Christ's power resides within her. The bride must remain faithful. She must continue to pursue the ministry opportunities she's given. She must hear the bridegroom's voice: *Put your trust in Me, beloved. Do not be afraid. I will protect you.*

Day Four
Reject & Resist

Yesterday we considered Jesus' messages to the persecuted church. Today we will examine a more subtle danger to Christ's bride—false teaching. We must learn to reject false teaching and resist impurity. The Bible clearly warns that false teachers are "among" us and that "many" will follow their shameful ways (2 Pet. 2:1-2). False teaching can come from both inside and outside the church. No matter its path of attack, false teaching is extremely dangerous and threatens the effectiveness of the bride's preparations.

THE MESSAGE TO THE CHURCH AT THYATIRA

Thyatira was known for its commerce—particularly a purple dye used to produce beautiful clothing. Many believe that Lydia, a dealer in purple cloth, helped establish the church there. That belief is partially founded on the Acts 16:14-15 account of Lydia's salvation. While the church was founded on the pure gospel taught by the disciples, the Thyatira congregation became polluted by false teaching.

Search the Scripture

> **Read Revelation 2:18-29. How did Jesus identify Himself in verse 18?**
> ○ as the One with the sharp, double-edged sword
> ◉ as the Son of God whose eyes are like fire and feet like bronze
> ○ as the Amen, the faithful and true witness

Interestingly, this is the only time in Revelation that Jesus used the designation Son of God. Perhaps this was in response to the city's preoccupation with the sun god, Apollo.[8] Whatever the reason, Jesus' description of one "whose eyes are like blazing fire and whose feet are like burnished bronze," speaks of judgment.[9]

> **What encouragements did Jesus offer the Thyatira church (v. 19)?**
>
> *I know you have grown in your love + faith + Service + perserverance*

> **Which of the following did Jesus have against "the woman, Jezebel"? (Draw a star by all that apply.)**
>
> Was a liar.   Misled servants into sexual immorality. ✓
> Acting like a man.   Taught Satan's deep secrets.
> Practiced witchcraft.   Encouraged eating food sacrificed to idols. ✓
> Was a false teacher. ✓   Unwilling to repent. ✓

The Thyatira church was busy. Unlike the church at Sardis, her busyness was more than religious activity. In fact, her growing ministry in the name of Christ clearly demonstrated love, faith, and perseverance (v. 19). Yet Jesus found something very disturbing in the Thyatira church. His bride permitted a false prophetess to teach false doctrine, leading believers into idolatry and sexual immorality. Under the influence of this so-called prophetess, the bride began to forget her bridegroom.

It's unlikely that the woman Jesus referred to in Revelation was actually named Jezebel. The name is probably symbolic, referring to the idolatrous Queen Jezebel who introduced Baal worship to Israel and enticed mass spiritual adultery as well as sexual immorality (see 1 Kings 16:31-33). But the Jezebel of the Thyatira church also wielded deadly power, claiming to be a prophetess and apparently coaxing members of the church away from Scripture's teachings. She convinced some that sexual perversion and pagan practices were acceptable to God.

Names carried special significance in Jewish life and were usually carefully chosen. To learn why it's unlikely that a Jewish family in New Testament times would have named their daughter Jezebel, see 1 Kings 16:31-33; 18:1-4; 19:1-6; 2 Kings 9:22,30.

Discover the Meaning

While the specific Jezebel mentioned in Jesus' address to Thyatira is long dead, similar false teachings are still a danger to the church. Not only do they interfere with preparations for the bridegroom's return, they also threaten the bride's purity. Therefore, the bride must stay alert, learning to quickly recognize and reject lies.

Who or what is the source of false teaching (2 Cor. 11:13-15)?
○ evil people   ○ human thinking   ◉ Satan

What three areas of false teaching does Jude 3-4 warn about?
◉ teaching that denies the deity of Christ
○ teaching that denies God created the world in seven days
◉ teaching that denies Jesus as Lord
◉ teaching that uses grace as a license for immorality

How can believers recognize false teaching (Col. 2:6-8)?
○ by listening to a variety of speakers with different ideas
◉ by weighing whether the message is based on basic world principles or on Christ
○ by asking a close friend

How should we test a teaching to determine if it's false (1 John 4:1-3)?

Every spirit that confesses that Jesus Christ has come in the flesh is from God. It is false teaching if it denies the truth that Jesus is LORD.

False teaching is Satan's tool. It denies the truth that Jesus is Lord. It corrupts the church by turning her away from the bridegroom's loving attention. The church has the responsibility of guarding against false teaching by leaning on Jesus, remaining faithful in Him, and strengthening her faith through reading His Word.

Make It Personal

Daily the world entices Christ's bride to compromise her relationship with her beloved. The church must realize that the world's false teaching always leads to spiritual adultery (see Jer. 3:6; Hos. 9:1). As we have learned, the bride has pledged eternal faithfulness to her bridegroom. Therefore, she must vigilantly guard against any teaching that doesn't build up her relationship with Christ.

How does your church guard against false teaching?

<u>Staying in God's Word</u>

What can you do to prevent false doctrine from taking root in your life and church? Read the Scriptures, beloved. Know what the Word of God says.

Interesting fact:

Considering that the church body need only look to parchments containing God's Word to understand her bridegroom's heart, I find it ironic that Pergamum was famous for its invention and manufacture of parchment. In fact, the Greek word for *parchment* is derived from Pergamum's name. How interesting that parchments contained the Word of God the church so desperately needed!

THE MESSAGE TO THE CHURCH AT PERGAMUM

Pergamum was known for its religion. In fact, the city housed some of the world's finest temples in which to honor their many gods.[10] In Revelation 2:13 Jesus referred to the city as "where Satan lives."

Search the Scripture

Read Revelation 2:12-17. How did Jesus identify Himself?
- ○ as the First and the Last
- ● as the One with the sharp, double-edged sword
- ○ as the holy and true

How did Jesus encourage the Pergamum church (v. 13)?

you did not deny my name

Like the church at Smyrna, the church at Pergamum suffered persecution yet remained true to Christ. In verse 13 Jesus offered encouragement by reminding His bride that He knows her suffering; He understands the challenges of living in a world where Satan is allowed to rule.

How could Jesus empathize with the church of Pergamum's situation?

_____

_____

What did Jesus have against the church at Pergamum (vv. 14-15)?

◉ false teaching   ○ requiring circumcision   ○ not standing for Him

Which of the following best sums up Jesus' instruction to this church?

○ Work harder!   ◉ Repent!   ○ Get ready for a fight!

Although the Pergamum church endured persecution in Christ's name, Jesus warned of a subtle threat. A group within the church compromised its faith by participating in pagan worship. These individuals apparently practiced idol worship that included sexually immoral behavior. Therefore, the bride—committed to remain pure, set apart, and holy—allowed herself to become defiled from within. The word *pergamum* means *married!*[11] How sad that a city whose name represented the bride's elevation to the holy marriage relationship with her beloved became so defiled!

Note that Jesus did not accuse the church of believing or teaching these false doctrines but of allowing them. Her sin was in refusing to confront the issue by speaking the truth in love. The bride failed to guard against lies, therefore compromising the precious gift of purity.

Discover the Meaning

To recognize a lie we must first understand truth. Jesus is the truth (John 14:6). Satan relentlessly entices the church to exchange the truth of Christ for the lies of the world (Rom. 1:25). Christ's bride must fight to remain steadfast in God's truth. The commitment to purity demands that she love truth and hate what Jesus hates.

Knowing the Word of God is essential to understanding what the bridegroom adores and despises. His Word reveals truth by exposing lies. Deception had polluted the church at Pergamum and only the power of truth could make her clean again. How exciting that the bridegroom sent her a personal and redeeming message: Repent and remain true!

Make It Personal

How does the situation in the Pergamum church demonstrate that sacrificial service cannot make up for tolerating evil?

_____

If you have ever encountered false teaching, how did you respond?

_____

Which of the following best illustrates how a church might "allow" false teaching without believing in the teaching?

○ by forbidding teaching by anyone but the pastor

○ by failing to adequately train teachers

◉ by not confronting a teacher who teaches contrary to God's Word

Why is it important that your church learn to effectively speak the truth in love?

_____

_____

The church must aggressively protect herself from the devastation of false teaching. Recognizing that false teachers will be among us, the bride must diligently compare all instruction to the Bible and she must ask her attendants to do the same. Jesus desires to protect His bride from those who would distract her from her preparations and seek to take away her joy. May we remain steadfastly grounded on the unchanging truth of who He is and what He has called us to do!

Day Five
Beware of Pride

When I was in the second grade, an observant teacher suspected that I suffered from poor eyesight. After school one day she asked me to read the eye chart in her classroom. To my horror I could only see the big letter "E"! Up until that moment I had no idea that my vision was impaired. Because my condition developed early and progressed slowly, I didn't realize how much my sight had deteriorated.

What a wonderful surprise when I put glasses on for the first time! I was amazed that I could actually see the individual leaves on trees. To this day I still thank that teacher for my dramatically improved vision.

Just as our sight can deteriorate over time, our spiritual vision can also become impaired. Like the physical variety, spiritual blindness can occur slowly and go unnoticed. The bride of Christ needs clear vision to complete her betrothal preparations. Poor spiritual vision will slow her down and eventually cause preparations to cease. Today's lesson offers an opportunity to examine the bride's spiritual vision and provides a check-up we all need. Together we'll consider one of the most common causes of spiritual blindness: pride. A short-sighted disease, pride distorts our focus on Jesus and sharpens our focus on ourselves.

MESSAGE TO THE CHURCH OF LAODICEA

Wealthy Laodicea was located at the intersection of three major roads, situated between a city famous for hot springs and a city known for its cold water. Part of Laodicea's wealth came from the production of a special eye salve[12]—a fact you may soon find ironic.

Search the Scripture

Read Revelation 3:14-22. How did Jesus identify Himself?

○ as the First and the Last

◉ as the Amen, the faithful and true witness

○ as the One who is holy and true

The word "Amen" means truth.[13] In verse 14 Jesus identified Himself as the faithful witness and the originator of all creation. As we've learned, Christ is the embodiment of divine truth, and His earthly life reflected it. Remember that as Jesus stood before Pilate, the ruler asked Him, "So You are a king?" (John 18:37, NASB). Jesus affirmed the accusation, adding that He was born to testify to that fact. How important it is that we not lose sight of the truth that Jesus is *the* King–ruler of every nation and all creation. As such, He was compelled to bear witness to the truth of the church of Laodicea's sinful condition.

What words of encouragement did Jesus offer (Rev. 3:19)?

those whom I love, I reprove & discipline
Be zealous & repent

Write Jesus' warning from verse 16.

Because you are lukewarm, neither hot nor cold, I will spit you out of My mouth.

What specific counsel did Jesus give in verse 18?

They needed the gold of God's glory and righteousness

Before we concentrate on the church at Laodicea's shortcomings, let's look at the touching encouragement Jesus offered her. Notice that in verse 19 He reminds her that He only disciplines those He loves. Proverbs 3:11-12 affirms His words: "Do not despise the Lord's discipline and do not resent his rebuke, because the Lord disciplines those He loves, as a father the son he delights in." Jesus' words to the church, though harsh, were not meant to condemn. Rather, they were meant to correct and to inspire the bride to run from harm.

As we've explored Jesus' messages to the other six churches, one thing became clear: None of them were perfect. Yet it seems that not one received a more severe rebuke than the church of Laodicea. Her condition personally offended Jesus.

Why did Jesus find the Laodicean church so offensive (Rev. 3:15)?

He wanted them to not be hot or cold but zealous w/ spiritual fervor
He wanted a burning flame

What spiritual temperatures do Luke 24:32 and Matthew 24:12 describe?

heart is burning   *love will grow cold*

According to Romans 12:11, the church should … (check one)
○ stay in the middle of the road to avoid upsetting people
● be full of spiritual fervor
○ be controlled and reserved

Jesus' harsh words of warning were necessary to communicate the grave reality of the church's spiritual condition. Deceived by pride and materialism, the Laodicea church depended on herself rather than Him. The divine bridegroom will not accept apathy and self-focus: They make Him sick.

THE ROOT OF THE PROBLEM

Search the Scripture

In Laodicea the church became so comfortable that she no longer saw her need. In fact, she became so self-satisfied and secure in her own resources that she thought she had everything under control and needed nothing. She pushed Jesus aside; she felt no need for Him.

Most likely her foolishness began as her values were infected by the wealthy culture surrounding her. Notice that immediately after telling the church that because of her spiritual temperature He would "spit" her out, Jesus added: "You say, 'I am rich; I have acquired wealth and do not need a thing' " (v. 17). Financial wealth had apparently become more important to her than spiritual health. As a result, she incorrectly measured her success based on material possession.

How did Jesus assess the Laodicean church's success (Rev. 3:17)?

You do not know you are wretched + miserable + poor + blind + naked

With this in mind, know that the church today must take care not to judge her success by human standards. Financial success promotes a value system contrary to God's. This worldly standard based on materialism can creep into the church in ways that seem harmless. For example, a mind-set that bigger is always better or the belief that we must have the newest technology to effectively minister can lead a church to spend more time and money on material resources than the development of spiritual ones. To remain pure, the bride must remember that true, lasting wealth comes from the Lord.

Read Matthew 13:22. According to this passage, which of the following chokes the Word, making believers unfruitful? (Check all that apply.)
● the deceitfulness of wealth   ○ evil thoughts
● the worries of this world   ○ the desire to reach others

Discover the Meaning

I believe Christ gave His bride two important lessons on spiritual economics. First, spiritual riches are not acquired by our works or material wealth. God's spiritual economy is based on divine grace. Its currency is faith and obedience. Depending on material wealth will spiritually bankrupt the bride of Christ; she must depend completely on the infinite spiritual wealth of her faithful bridegroom.

The second spiritual lesson closely ties to the first. The church at Laodicea, apparently pleased with her own success, developed a big pride problem as her riches increased. Pride blinds us to our shortcomings, making us spiritually weak and ineffective. The church's pride was a sin that cost her dearly. Her spiritual growth ceased, and she became unfruitful. She was so wrapped up in herself that she neglected her bridegroom, treating Him with indifference.

Read John 15:5. What can we do apart from Christ?

nothing

Pride reaps unpleasant consequences. What do these Scriptures say about pride?

Proverbs 16:18 _Pride goes before destruction_

2 Timothy 3:1-2 _In the last days, men will be lovers of self & money, arrogant & boastful, disobedient to parents, unholy & ungrateful_

1 John 2:16 _the boastful pride of life is not from the Father, but from the world_

Jesus fervently instructed the church to repent of her sin. But true repentance requires her to humble herself before her bridegroom, acknowledging the folly of materialism and pride. Jesus knocked on the door of the church's heart, offering to fan her lukewarm coals into a burning flame. She had a decision to make. Would she humbly open the door to let Him back in?

Make It Personal

The Laodicean church was so infatuated with the world and so comfortable in her wealth that she was blind to her own foolishness. She could neither see herself as she really was nor her bridegroom knocking on her heart's door. Only intimate relationship with her bridegroom could heal her spiritual blindness (see Rev. 3:18).

Are areas of your life infatuated with the world? ○ yes ○ no ○ not sure
If you marked yes, ask God to reveal to you any blind spots in your life.
Invite Him to heal you.

As we conclude our look at Jesus' messages to His bride, please take a moment to review this week's lessons. Ask Christ to reveal hidden dangers threatening your church and your walk with Him. Hear His call as He walks among the churches, "Repent and be cleansed! Beloved, the divine wedding day draws near!"

meet
7/25/2011

for
Barbara
Joyce
Cheri
Carol
Betty

The Bridegroom's Return

(6)

I RECENTLY RECEIVED WONDERFUL NEWS. My oldest daughter, Amber, and her husband, Keith, are expecting their second child. I'm going to be a grandma again! These days our whole family is anxiously awaiting the arrival of our newest member. We know that the baby's coming will bring a time of great joy as we once again celebrate God's miracle of life. In the meantime, wondering about the baby's gender, hair color, and precise day of arrival only increases our anticipation as we see signs that the time is growing closer.

Our excitement is expressed in eager preparations—converting a guest room, buying diapers, and acquiring new-baby essentials. We're also trying to clear our calendars, earnestly preparing to be present for the blessed arrival whether the baby comes at due date or two weeks prior like big brother Jared. Whenever the child comes, we know we'll find such joy in personally welcoming him or her into our family! None of us want to miss a moment of the joyful event!

You and I have received the good news of the divine bridegroom's impending return and the immeasurable joy His coming will bring. Christ's bride and her faithful attendants have been called to prepare for His arrival. As the wedding date draws ever closer, the urgency of our preparations intensifies. And so should the level of our excitement.

Day One

The Celebration Is Coming

It's hard to believe we've arrived at the last week of our journey together. I must admit, I have mixed emotions as I sit down to type this final chapter. On one hand, I wish our adventure wasn't ending so soon. On the other, I've long and anxiously awaited our look at the return of Christ. This glimpse of the divine bridegroom's breathtaking approach makes me want to shout for joy! I hope it will have a similar effect on you.

Before we begin, let's press the rewind button one last time as we briefly review the kingdom calendar.

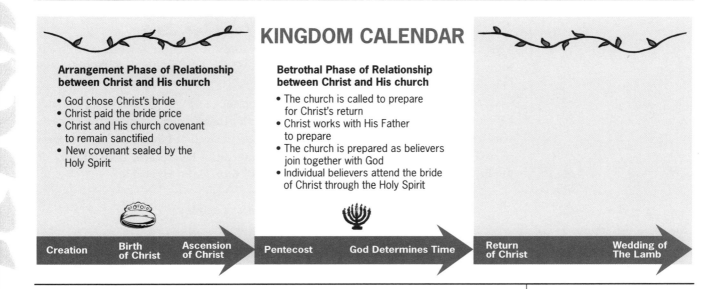

KINGDOM CALENDAR

Arrangement Phase of Relationship between Christ and His church
- God chose Christ's bride
- Christ paid the bride price
- Christ and His church covenant to remain sanctified
- New covenant sealed by the Holy Spirit

Betrothal Phase of Relationship between Christ and His church
- The church is called to prepare for Christ's return
- Christ works with His Father to prepare
- The church is prepared as believers join together with God
- Individual believers attend the bride of Christ through the Holy Spirit

| Creation | Birth of Christ | Ascension of Christ | Pentecost | God Determines Time | Return of Christ | Wedding of The Lamb |

Biblical Background

You'll remember from week 1 that the final stage of the Jewish marriage process is the celebration phase. Formally called the *nissuin*, it usually occurred about one year after the betrothal ceremony.[1] The festivities began upon the bridegroom's return for his beloved and encompassed the much-anticipated wedding celebration that was among the most joyous events in Jewish life.

As you may recall, *nissuin* comes from the Hebrew verb *nasa*, which means "to be carried off, lifted up."[2] This definition is fitting; surely both the bride and groom felt carried away with excitement and joy as the big day arrived. For today's study it's also important to note that one dictionary further defines *nasa* as "graciously received, held in honour."[3] That addition well describes the proud, loving look in the groom's eyes the first moment he sees his radiant bride on their wedding day!

Throughout ancient Jewish history, the bridegroom's return brought honor to the bride, elevating her to a new life with her beloved. Her preparations complete, her longing at an end, the bride's dreams finally became a reality. Likewise, when Christ returns, His precious bride will be lifted up out of this sinful world. In a dramatic demonstration of God's gracious forgiveness, Christ will lovingly honor His church by affectionately elevating her to new and everlasting life.

Our dreams of locking our eyes with Christ's and of pleasing Him through faithful preparation will all be accomplished on His glorious return. My heart beats in wild anticipation as I consider the coming divine celebration!

JESUS WILL RETURN

Search the Scripture

Earlier, I asked you to write John 14:1-3 and carry it with you. Hopefully, you've memorized it. Summarize Jesus' promise in the passage.

Jesus said
I go to prepare a place for you + Jesus is coming back to take us to that place

Christ's return will always generate discussion and speculation. But one fact is clear: Jesus said He would return, and He will. I pray that fact is forever burned in your heart and mind!

We know many believers have lost focus on the reality of Christ's reappearance. Like the church at Sardis, some bury the truth of His second coming under cares and constant activities. Others, like those of the church at Laodicea, have become so infatuated with the world they have lost interest in His return. Dear Friend, do not be deceived or distracted. Jesus Christ will soon claim His bride!

Are you living in daily anticipation of Christ's coming?
○ no   ● yes   ○ sometimes   ○ I'm not sure.

Beloved, if you answered anything other than "yes," be advised that you are in danger of falling prey to one of Satan's best tactics for distracting us in our preparations and turning our love for Christ cold.

According to 2 Peter 3:3-4, what can we expect the world to say about the promise of Jesus' coming?

Mocking
Where is the promises of His coming?
Why isn't He here yet?

"So where is this Jesus you claim is coming?" "Why isn't He here yet?" "Maybe He's forgotten you." "It could be that all that second-coming talk is just a myth your Sunday school teacher made up!" These are only a few of the taunts used to pull Christians away from their preparations, making some doubt the certainty of Christ's return. And if you've never been confronted with one of these, you will be. We must have a ready response to such questions that will protect us from doubt.

Keeping all you've learned about Christ's coming in mind, read 2 Peter 3:8-9,14-15. Then mark the following statements true (T) or false (F).
_T_ God's concept of time is different from ours.
_T_ Believers and the church should focus on being prepared for Christ's return.

_F_ If Christ delays in coming, it may mean He has changed His mind.

_T_ Christ's patience provides opportunity for salvation.

Imagine a Christian friend has just expressed she doubts whether Christ is really coming back. Write your response to her in the margin.

Discover the Meaning

Throughout our study we've explored the relationship between the timing of Christ's return and His bride's state of readiness. As I consider all we've learned about their relationship, I picture a young man standing at the foot of the staircase in the home of his future in-laws. Upstairs his bride-to-be leisurely prepares for their afternoon outing, exchanging her red sweater for the blue and gazing dreamily at the picture of her fiancé. But at her mother's announcement that the young man has arrived, the girl swiftly grabs her purse and practically runs to meet him. Somehow the knowledge that he's waiting for her greatly speeds her preparation.

Patiently, Jesus waits for His bride to make herself ready for His return. I believe that the church's sensitivity to that reality greatly affects her state of readiness. The more conscious the bride is of her beloved's coming, the greater her motivation to diligently prepare to meet Him. It's not enough that the divine bride simply prepare for Christ's return; she must also eagerly long for and look for His arrival.

ANTICIPATING HIS APPEARANCE

Search the Scripture

In Matthew 22:1-13 Jesus again compares the kingdom to the ancient marriage experience. In the parable of the wedding banquet, He reminds us of the great honor of being invited to the celebration and the eternal consequence of refusing God's gracious invitation. Perhaps most significant to this week's lesson, this parable sheds light on the final phase of the ancient Jewish marriage experience.

Read Matthew 22:1-13. Who determined the date and time of the wedding celebration?

the father

Remember what we learned in week 2: God alone—much like the father in the parable of the wedding banquet—has the authority to determine the date of His Son's return. Even Jesus does not know the specific time. Only when God the Father is satisfied that everything is ready will He send His Son to claim the bride. In that moment—in that second—the heavenly celebration will begin.

Even considering what we've discovered about God's divine patience in giving the bride time to complete her preparations, you may still struggle with the secrecy surrounding the exact date. Even the disciples, at the brink of Christ's ascension, wanted to know *when* Jesus would return (see Acts 1:6-7). Thankfully, Jesus gave the disciples something far more valuable than a date to mark on their calendars. He gave them a greater understanding of their purpose during His absence: they were to faithfully prepare themselves and others for His coming (Acts 1:7-8).

You see, it's not just that we don't know the date of Christ's return but that we don't need to know. The timing of the divine bridegroom's appearance is simply irrelevant to the call to diligently prepare and make ready for the coming wedding. Our responsibility as attendants is to remain focused on the truth that the divine bridegroom will return instead of becoming distracted by speculations as to precisely when He will arrive.

As I consider the preoccupation some believers have with predicting Christ's coming, I'm reminded of my childhood. When my mother first began working outside our home, she assigned each of us after-school chores. Invariably, we waited to do these tasks until the very last minute, quickly and sloppily finishing as my mother drove into the driveway. Every afternoon we called her at work to ask when she was coming home, idly delaying our housework as long as possible. In truth, we really didn't need to know when Mother was coming; we needed to do what she asked of us.

> **Read Matthew 24:45-51. Explain the reasoning behind the servant's bad behavior (v. 48).**

My master is not coming for a long time so I have time to do as I please.

> **How does this parable relate to the return of Christ?**
> ○ It shows why we should be cautious of trusting church leaders.
> ● It shows what can happen if we cease expecting Christ's return.
> ○ It shows that many will suffer before Christ returns.

Discover the Meaning

First John 2:28 says that we should remain in Christ so that when He returns we can be confident and unashamed. As I recall my own guilty feelings when my mother–who trusted me to complete my assigned tasks faithfully–came home, I can certainly see the wisdom in this passage. Looking and longing for the bride-groom's return, instead of giving Him only an occasional passing thought during a sermon, inspires faithfulness to Him and to His call to readiness. When we cease to expect His return, we lose our sense of purpose. Like the disobedient servant, the believer and the church that cease to expect Jesus' return become worldly, dishon-oring the bridegroom and possibly even mistreating others. Scripture admonishes us to "remain in Him." In doing so, we will never lose focus on Christ.

> **What does 2 Timothy 4:8 promise those who long for Christ's return?**

The Crown of righteousness

For those who live for Jesus and steadfastly long for His coming, eternal reward is promised. How appropriate that our reward for faithful preparation is called a "crown of righteousness." It is awarded in recognition of the righteousness we have allowed God to accomplish in our lives. Beloved, if you longingly prepare for Christ's appearing—obediently allowing God to work in and through you—you will receive a glorious crown!

Make it Personal

How do the assurance of the divine celebration and of a crown of righteousness contribute to your commitment to preparing the bride?

_____

I've always believed Christ would return, yet I'm only just beginning to learn how to expectantly live each day in full assurance of this fact. Dear friend, learning to daily live in the light of the certainty of Christ's return is a process. With God's help, I'm more aware this week of Christ's return and the preparations needed than I was last. I pray that next week I will experience an even greater awareness of His coming. I want my single-minded desire and preparation for His return to become a holy habit, moving me ever closer to the moment when I'll humbly receive my glorious crown of righteousness. I also want to watch you get your crown and join with the throng of other faithful attendants in celebrating God's greatness.

How is this study increasing your certainty of Christ's return?
How has it affected your personal preparations?

_____

Beloved, the divine bridegroom's return is imminent—He could come at any moment! Longing for His return and expectantly living and preparing for that glorious time will bring rewards and celebration beyond our imaginations.
Anticipate the joy of gazing into the eyes of our Savior.

Day Two
The Trumpet Will Sound

A young pastor's daughter recently explained her childhood terror at finding herself home alone. One afternoon her father had momentarily stepped out into the backyard, and her mother was cleaning out the attic. As the girl awoke from a nap, the house seemed completely empty. No one was in the living room or kitchen. No one

Revelation 4:9-11 describes believers laying their crowns before God in an act of heavenly worship. To learn more about the other crowns available to believers, see James 1:12 (the crown of life); 1 Peter 5:4 (the crown of glory); and Revelation 2:10 (the martyr's crown).

"Therefore
KEEP WATCH,
because you do not know
WHAT DAY YOUR
LORD WILL COME.
So you also must
be ready, because
THE SON OF MAN
WILL COME
at an hour when you
do not expect him."
MATTHEW 24:42,44

in the bedrooms, bathrooms, or basement. Worse, her father's half-eaten bagel and half-empty coffee cup sat on the dining room table—apparently deserted. Though the girl had committed her heart to the Lord, she admits, "I was so scared that day. I honestly thought Jesus had come back and left me behind!"

Yesterday's lesson emphasized believing in and longing for Christ's return. Today we'll explore biblical truths concerning His coming. These truths will help dispel doubts and fears that threaten to rob us of the sense of overwhelming expectation the bridegroom's exciting return naturally brings. Hopefully, what we learn today will prevent any of us from having our own scary "left behind" moments.

Biblical Background

Let's return to the parable of the wedding banquet to uncover more clues concerning the final phase of the ancient Jewish marriage experience.

> **Review Matthew 22:1-13. What does verse 3 reveal about those to whom the message was sent?**
> ● They had already received an invitation to the banquet.
> ○ They were all wealthy.
> ○ They did not have the proper clothes to wear to the celebration.

In ancient times the father of the bridegroom issued two separate wedding invitations. The first alerted guests to the upcoming wedding celebration without giving the exact date (Matt. 22:2-3). I believe this first invitation corresponds to God's invitation to salvation. This first announcement not only built anticipation throughout the community but also served notice to the bride: "Hurry! Your bridegroom will soon arrive!" Only when the father determined that everything was fully prepared was the second invitation issued. It immediately summoned the guests to the wedding celebration (see Matt. 22:2-3).

LISTENING FOR HIS RETURN

Though the parable of the wedding banquet does not mention this detail, my research revealed that a *shofar* or trumpet was often sounded to assemble the guests for an ancient wedding celebration. At its call, the bridegroom "would lead a wedding procession through the streets of the village to the house of the bride."[4] Accompanied by his friends and amid singing and music, the bridegroom led the group through the streets of the town to the bride's home. Along the way, friends who were ready and waiting with their lamps lit would join the procession. Veiled and dressed in beautifully embroidered clothes and adorned with jewels, the bride, accompanied by her attendants, joined the bridegroom for the advance to his father's house.[5] Sometimes the Jewish bridegroom returned for his bride late at night.[6] Because of this, the bridegroom's loud shout as the wedding procession began was sometimes called "the midnight cry" (Matt. 25:6). Understand that I'm not suggesting Jesus will come when our clocks strike midnight, although He may. However, I do believe He will return to claim His bride during a time of great spiritual darkness.

In 2 Timothy 3:1-5, Paul describes the increasing spiritual darkness of the last days. All around us today we see evidence of what Paul describes. Many love themselves above others, the family unit is under siege, and we find an escalating lack of self-control throughout our culture. But perhaps most frightening of all is the darkness experienced by those who have a form of godliness (outward appearance of religion) yet deny its power to change their lives. Times are indeed growing more evil, and the world around us appears to be in total chaos. As believers, we must take care not to let all the noise of this chaos distract us from our preparations or from listening for the second wedding invitation.

Search the Scripture

Sounds remind us of particular life experiences. Church bells remind us of a recent wedding ceremony. A ship's horn evokes the memory of a romantic cruise. Music from an ice cream truck prompts recollections of lazy summers gone by. As a child I always associated Christ's return with a loud noise. I'm not sure if my understanding came from a Sunday School teacher or my own imagination. Regardless, whenever I heard an unusual or unfamiliar sound, my first thought was, *Jesus is coming!*

What three sounds will accompany Christ's return (1 Thess. 4:16-17)?

① A Shout from Jesus - command ② The Voice of the Archangel
③ trumpet of God

When Jesus returns, at whatever time He does, He will give a loud command or midnight cry that even those in the grave will hear (John 5:28). The sound of His voice will command those dead in Him to rise.

The voice of the archangel will follow. And while scholars disagree on the exact meaning of the archangel's voice in this passage, it's worth mentioning that in Bible times a member of the bridegroom's procession customarily shouted, "Behold, the bridegroom comes!"[7] Perhaps the archangel, like an excited and anxious grooms- man, will be given the honor of shouting the thrilling announcement of the heavenly bridegroom's return. (Just imagining the scene makes me want to shout!)

What did Paul mean by the "trumpet call of God" (1 Thess. 4:16)?

_____

First Thessalonians explains that as Jesus' command echoes across the earth, the archangel's voice and the trumpet blast reverberate behind it. That trumpet call always seemed anticlimactic to me until I discovered that in Bible times, people understood it represented more than just a musical tune.

Read Numbers 10:1-3,9-10. Explain in the margin how the children ① breaking camp
of Israel were to use and respond to the trumpet's call.

② all the congregation shall gather themselves @ the tent of meeting
③ as a call to war for God to protect them from their enemies

Read Exodus 19:16-20. What did the children of Israel do in response to God's loud trumpet blast? (Check all that apply.)

○ trembled   ○ stayed in their tents   ◉ gathered to meet with God

I believe the "trumpet call of God" mentioned in 1 Thessalonians represents the trumpet sounded at God's command, a fact solidified by the important role the *shofar* played in Jewish life during Bible times. Basically, the blowing of the *shofar* signaled change to the Jew. It sounded when it was time to move on (Num. 10:5-6). It announced the arrival of holy days and signaled the beginning of battle (Num. 10:9-10). With this in mind, it comes as no surprise that humanity's most miraculous change will take place when the final trumpet sounds.

Read 1 Corinthians 15:51-52.

Discover the Meaning

In the twinkling of an eye, Christ will gather His bride and take her home. Just as the trumpet's call brought God's people together in the day of Moses, so too will it bring them together on the day of the bridegroom's glorious return. Saints of all nations and all races, speaking every imaginable language, will rise to meet their divine bridegroom in the air. My friend, that day is coming quickly!

Turn back to 1 Thessalonians 4:16-17. According to verse 16, who will rise first when Christ returns?

<u>the dead in Christ</u>

According to verse 17, what will happen to those who are still alive?

Believers who remain <u>will be caught up together w/ them in the clouds to meet the Lord in the air + so we shall always be w/ the Lord</u> *the dead believers*

Read 1 Corinthians 15:35-42. To what does Paul compare this mass resurrection of the dead in verses 35-37?

○ reconstructive surgery   ◉ growing a plant from a seed
○ resurrection of Lazarus from the dead

The "dead in Christ" are the physical bodies of believers who experience physical death before Christ's return. Paul compared the resurrection of the perishable human body to seeds growing into plants. Dead bodies are the planted seeds, and resurrected bodies are the glorious flowers that come from the seeds. When Christ returns, the perishable physical bodies will be raised to new, imperishable bodies.

According to 2 Corinthians 5:6-8, where does the soul of the believer go after physical death?

<u>absent from the dead body and home w/the Lord!</u>

When we die our souls do not remain with our bodies: to be out of our bodies is to be present with the Lord (2 Cor. 5:8). At his or her physical death, a believer's soul is immediately transported into Christ's presence. But when Jesus returns, He will bring with Him the souls of those who have died.

Imagine the mass of individuals involved in the incredible reunion of Christ and His bride! Both the dead in Christ and those alive at His return will meet Him in the air. All believers receive their new spiritual bodies upon the bridegroom's coming (1 Cor. 15:51-52). Together they become the transformed bride who joins the heavenly procession dressed and ready for the divine wedding celebration.

Make It Personal

Our belief in Christ's return is vital to fulfilling our divine purpose. Satan wants to deceive and discourage us concerning Christ's approach. He will play on our fears of the unknown and will raise doubts about the truth of Christ's second coming. Preparing ourselves to combat those doubts and fears with God's Word is critical.

Perhaps you believe in Jesus but need help in believing in His return. If so, pray that the Holy Spirit will help you with your unbelief.

One day the bride of Christ will hear the bridegroom's approach. At His call, she and her faithful attendants will join in a heavenly procession, joyfully ascending to her new home with Him.

Stay alert, Beloved. Continue preparing and keep listening!

Day Three
Unspeakable Joy

I've always loved young children's joy and excitement! My favorite home movies include my children's preschool Christmas programs. One year my daughter, Katie, was so caught up in the joy of the moment that she tried to sing her friend's solo and almost forgot her own! She sang with all she had—belting out each line with enthusiasm and punctuating the song with hand motions. By the end of that program, the golden tinsel belt holding up Katie's angel costume had fallen from her waist down to her ankles! But she sang on, unconcerned. I will never forget the look of sheer joy on her face as she sang, "Emmanuel!" at the top of her sweet little voice.

Today we'll consider the incomparable joy that Christ's return will bring. I believe the better we understand the divine bridegroom's glorious appearance, the more readily we will prepare His bride. When the divine wedding of the Lamb begins, the heavenly procession's joy will reach an eternal crescendo.

I pray today's lesson will quicken our preparations—and our pulses—as we are encouraged by the incredible joy before us.

Biblical Background

Though most of us consider weddings to be joyous events, we must understand that great celebration literally defined the Jewish bridegroom's return in Bible times. As we've learned, all who joined in the bridal proceedings were expected to add to the joy of the bride and groom. Shouts of joy and excitement only intensified as the procession celebrating the groom's return ended and the wedding feast began.

The Jewish people have long been known for their outward demonstrations of joy, including music, singing, dancing, and playing games; it's easy to imagine the Jewish wedding scene as a wonderful time of fun and excitement. People laughing. Children playing. Guests singing and dancing. The jubilant celebration usually lasted seven days (Gen. 29:27; Judg. 14:12). Without a doubt, community-wide elation ran high during that week.

Psalm 45:10-15 confirms the great joy of the Jewish wedding celebration. Some scholars believe this passage is a poetic description of the joyful process leading to the celebration of the wedding of Christ and His bride.

> **Read Psalm 45:10-15. According to verse 15, how are the bride and her attendants led out to meet the bridegroom?**

They will be led forth w/ gladness + rejoicing

Search the Scripture

> **With the picture of celebration fresh in your mind, carefully reread Revelation 19:6-9. According to this passage, how will the wedding of the Lamb begin?**
> ○ with heavenly music   ● with heavenly praise and worship
> ○ with a reading from God's Word   ○ with a moment of silence

Did you notice the divine wedding celebration begins with heavenly worship: Billions of voices singing, "Hallelujah! Our Lord God Almighty reigns!"? Each time I read this, I glow with anticipation of the bridegroom's return: I can hardly wait to join the waterfall of praise. How I hope this passage has a similar affect on you!

> **Write Revelation 19:7 in the margin.**

Isn't it interesting that heavenly praise and worship is accompanied by a call to great joy? The Greek word used for "be glad" (NIV) in this passage is *agalliao* which means, "to rejoice greatly, to exult."[8] Through research I discovered that *agalliao* implies a visible demonstration of great joy that includes skipping, dancing, and leaping.[9] It literally means jumping for joy!

Let's apply this concept to our understanding of the heavenly celebration. Imagine the bride, her attendants, and all of heaven rejoicing and being glad—openly demonstrating unspeakable joy at the wedding of Christ and His bride.

Rev 19:7

Let us rejoice and be glad and give the glory to Him, for the marriage of the Lamb has come and His bride has made herself ready

Close your eyes and picture yourself in this scene. Describe how you might outwardly display the joy of the divine celebration.

_____

_____

Discover the Meaning

You'll recall that earlier in our study we considered the modern bride, radiant in her love for the bridegroom and his love for her. But in ancient times, perhaps the *greatest* joy of the marriage celebration was seen in the bridegroom, whose rejoicing over his bride was legendary among the Jewish community.

To what does God compare the bridegroom's rejoicing (Isa. 62:5)?
○ the way a bride rejoices over her wedding garments
○ the birth of a child   ● how He rejoices over His people

How does this comparison help you better understand the joy of the wedding of the Lamb?

_____

I believe God used the rejoicing bridegroom to illustrate the joy He has for His people and to provide valuable insight into the heavenly joy that awaits Christ's bride. On the day of the divine wedding celebration, the bride's joy will not be one-sided. Jesus will rejoice over the church. Perhaps He will demonstrate His joy with singing (Zeph. 3:17). Perhaps He will dance or shout.

How will His beloved bride respond? One can only imagine.

UNINTERRUPTED JOY

Search the Scripture

Read Jeremiah 7:34; 25:10. What does God say about the joy and gladness of the wedding celebration?
○ Wedding celebrations are too joyous for the Sabbath.
● The destruction of Israel will be so great that there will be no more sounds of the joy and gladness of the wedding celebration.
○ He would never take away the joy and gladness of the wedding celebration.

Israel's blatant disobedience in forsaking God and worshiping what their hands had made resulted in harsh judgment from God (see Jer. 1:16). The Lord used the loss of gladness surrounding the wedding celebration to describe the extent of Israel's destruction. This image forced listeners to contemplate joy's devastating absence. Early listeners understood that if even the delighted voices of the bride and groom were silenced, the land itself must surely be a desolate waste. The disobedient nation of Israel faced retribution so overwhelming that the joyful sounds of wedding celebrations would no longer meet the ears of her people.

Read Jeremiah 33:10-11. What is the first sign of Israel's restoration?

the voice of joy + the voice of gladness

In Isaiah 25:6-9, the prophet Isaiah foretells God's restoration of His people and visualizes the divine wedding feast.

Losing the joy of the wedding celebration represented Israel's destruction. Joy's return symbolized its restoration. Be assured—the restoration of Christ's bride will result in unsurpassed celebration. Because the bride of Christ is not yet perfect, her own disobedience and the scars from fierce battles she has fought against evil require healing. All of heaven will rejoice over her eternal transformation. On that day, the bride of Christ will be made perfect (1 Cor. 15:51; Col. 1:22-28; Jude 1:24).

I can hardly wait to experience the special joy of the divine marriage celebration. I realize, however, that much remains to be done in preparing for the Lamb's glorious wedding. We mustn't allow Satan to discourage and distract us from worshiping, instructing, fellowshipping, and evangelizing. Though sometimes discouragement and distraction seem too great to overcome, we can face them with confidence. The writer of Hebrews offers valuable guidance in how to avoid being discouraged or distracted in our preparations.

Explain to what the "race marked out for us" refers (Heb. 12:1-3).

Fulfilling God's purpose for our lives, preparing for Christ's return by laying aside all encumbrances and sin following His example. Considering Jesus who endured the hostilities and the cross, and do not grow weary + lose heart. Rejoice in our preparations to meet Him.

What is the key to successfully completing this race (v. 2)?
- ○ training harder
- ◉ keeping our eyes on Jesus
- ○ asking others for help

The joy of seeing Jesus' face as He sees the joy in my face.

Today Christ's bride and her attendants prepare for and anticipate Jesus' return. As we work and wait, we must faithfully run the "race marked out for us," living out an illustration which refers to fulfilling God's purpose for our lives. Only when we fix our eyes on Christ and follow His example will we have the perseverance we need to fulfill God's plans for us. We must follow Christ's example of faithful endurance.

As we've discovered, Hebrews 12:2 explains that Jesus endured the cross "for the joy set before him." While I'm sure Christ anticipated reunion with His Father and His return to the throne, I'm equally sure another joy lay heavily on His mind as He endured the cross: the thought of His bride—made righteous by His sacrifice.

Recall that Jesus' shame, suffering, and death were part of the bride price He willingly paid. With this in mind, I believe that "the joy" mentioned in this verse refers to His excitement over reunion with the fully prepared bride: a wife who is clean, pure, and fully ready to meet Him.

Friends, this same joy that encouraged Jesus in the most difficult time of His earthly ministry is before us today, encouraging us during inevitable hardships and disappointments that come as we prepare for His return. We may face hurts now, but one day there will be no more pain. We may struggle now, but one day, the striving will cease. We may grieve now, but one day the grieving will end. In Christ we can endure and, one day, we will experience uninterrupted joy!

I don't know about you, but I've had days when I've been tempted to give up on the race. But God is teaching me to keep my eyes on Jesus; as I do, I am encouraged by the thought of the joy that awaits me when He returns. How I long to see the joy on the divine bridegroom's face as He sees the joy in mine!

Make It Personal

Beloved, you and I have received invitations to the wedding of the Lamb! As close friends of the bridegroom, part of the bride, and devoted attendants, we will definitely share in heaven's jubilant celebration! Remember that at the marriage supper, individual believers are guests, but collectively they are the bride of Christ.[10] Rejoice and be glad for our bridegroom is coming soon!

Close your eyes and imagine the wedding of the Lamb.
What do you most eagerly anticipate about the divine event?

Rejoicing in Christ's presence
Seeing His love for me
Going home to the new heaven + earth
Peace and joy

Christ's return and the heavenly celebration of His marriage to His church will be a time of unparalleled elation, but we don't have to wait until that moment to experience divine delight. God's presence is the source of all divine joy (Ps. 16:11). Experiencing His presence today reminds us of the greater joy that awaits us, giving us strength to press on.

Think about the last time you simply enjoyed being in God's presence—
no agendas, no requests, no complaints—just resting in Him. In the
margin, describe what those moments were like. Explain where you
were, how you responded to Him, and what you most remember.

For some of us, a long time has passed since we practiced the discipline of enjoying God's presence. Beloved, if you can't remember the last time you let everything go and simply enjoyed spending time with God, do not be discouraged. It's not too late. He is waiting for you.

As we conclude today's lesson, take time to experience afresh the awesome presence of almighty God. Talk to Him. Sing to Him. Delight in Him. Allow Him to fill you with His joy and find comfort in the fact that the greatest peace and joy He provides us on earth is only a taste of what's to come.

Day Four
The Most Perfect Union

Before we begin today's lesson, let's update the kingdom calendar to reflect what we've learned about the celebration phase of Christ's relationship with His church.

Match the spiritual reality with the corresponding elements of the celebration phase.

Spiritual Realities of Christ's Relationship with Church

1. _D_ God the Father decides everything is ready.
2. _C_ God sends Christ to claim His bride.
3. _A_ The trumpet will sound.
4. _B_ The divine wedding celebration begins.

Jewish Marriage Experience

(a) procession begins with blowing of shofar
(b) wedding celebration begins
(c) father sends his son to get his bride
(d) bridegroom's father decides everything is ready

Place the spiritual realities represented in the celebration phase on the kingdom calendar illustration below.

KINGDOM CALENDAR

Arrangement Phase of Relationship between Christ and His church

- God chose Christ's bride
- Christ paid the bride price
- Christ and His church covenant to remain sanctified
- New covenant sealed by the Holy Spirit

Creation | Birth of Christ | Ascension of Christ

Betrothal Phase of Relationship between Christ and His church

- The church is called to prepare for Christ's return
- Christ works with His Father to prepare
- The church is prepared as believers join together with God
- Individual believers attend the bride of Christ through the Holy Spirit

Pentecost | God Determines Time

Celebration Phase of Relationship between Christ and His church

God the Father decides everything is ready
God sends Christ to claim His bride
The trumpet will sound
The divine wedding celebration begins.

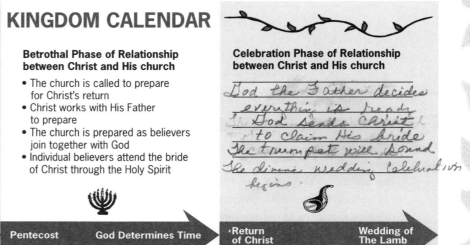

Return of Christ | Wedding of The Lamb

Have you ever met a couple who seemed to be a perfect match? I know one particular pair who seem to have a perfect relationship. They love the Lord and each other. They like the same activities and enjoy serving God together. The more Roger and I get to know them, the more apparent God's work in their lives becomes. While they are not perfect people, this couple has allowed God to create a near perfect union between them—not because they are perfect, but because He is.

You will recognize many of the Scriptures in today's lesson because we've studied them before. I hope, however, you will see them from a new perspective as we consider the final moments of divine transformation. Please resist the temptation to rush through these passages. They hold undiscovered treasure that will lead us to deeper understanding of the final steps in the bride of Christ's preparation!

Search the Scripture

Read Ephesians 5:25-27. Which of the following best describes the bride's condition upon her presentation to the divine bridegroom?
○ strong   ● perfected   ○ healthy

Which of the following does Jude 1:24 reveal about the church?
○ The church will never be perfect.
○ We will have made ourselves perfect by the time Christ returns.
● Christ will complete the perfection of the church and present her to Himself with great joy.

Why must Christ's bride be presented to Him holy and without fault? *He Wants us to be transformed + prepared for His return. Because Christ loved the church and gave Himself up for her*

Since her formation, the church has been in the process of divine transformation that will continue until Christ returns. In week 3 we saw two portraits of the church as displayed in Scripture—one as she presently is and the other as she will become. Just as when we stared into our mirrors as little girls and tried to envision ourselves as women, we often look at the church as she is rather than what she will become. Yet Jesus sees every dimension of His precious bride's transformation. He sees her as she once was, as she is now, and as she will become. Seeing the church as Jesus sees her may help us better understand the divine change process and gives us confidence she will be made perfect.

Remember that the church's future is eternally secure (Matt. 16:18). Even though Christ's bride may stumble, she will not fall. However, she is a living body that must be nurtured and guided toward her goal. The steadfast devotion of her faithful attendants result in changed lives, furthering the process of divine transformation of the bride. As we join together in community for worship, instruction, fellowship, and evangelism, God continues to transform the church into the perfected bride of Christ. Each step of transformation makes her more prepared for the return of her beloved bridegroom who will instantly complete what He began (1 Cor. 15:51-52).

Lasting transformation is not always easy. In many ways, the church is like a caterpillar preparing to emerge from her cocoon. To become a beautiful butterfly she must strain and struggle. The exertion is a vital part of her metamorphosis from a lowly caterpillar to a lovely butterfly; without it the transformation cannot be completed. Likewise, the church experiences struggles as she and her attendants strain to cooperate with God and each other in the ongoing process of transformation from a group of sinful people to a beautifully radiant bride. These struggles can sometimes leave us frustrated and discouraged.

"Husbands, love your wives, just as **CHRIST LOVED THE CHURCH** *AND GAVE HIMSELF UP FOR HER to make her holy, cleansing her by the washing with water through the word, and to present her to himself as* **A RADIANT CHURCH,** *without stain or wrinkle or any other blemish, but* **HOLY AND BLAMELESS."** EPHESIANS 5:25-27

Like many of you, I've been discouraged at times and wanted to give up on preparing and investing in the church. I often feel incapable of giving Christ's bride the attention and time she needs to prepare. But when this happens I remind myself that I'm depending on my own efforts instead of trusting God's miraculous power. I'm learning that God is the source of all lasting transformation and the bride and her faithful attendants can and will be transformed in spite of our present shortcomings.

Read 1 John 3:1-3. According to verse 2, what two things will happen when Christ returns for His bride?

Christ will appear and we will be like Him and we will see Him as He is.

What does verse 3 tell us about what we are to do until Christ returns?
- ○ We're to attend conferences and Bible studies.
- ● We're to purify ourselves, becoming more like Him.
- ○ We are to make new clothes so we'll be ready.

This passage refers to each of the three phases of Christ's relationship with His church. We see evidence of the arrangement phase in verse 1, which emphasizes the extraordinary love of God lavished on us when He chose us to be a part of Christ's bride. God loved us enough to sacrifice His own Son to secure our future. Verse 3 refers to the betrothal phase, reminding us that Christ's bride must remain pure just as her beloved is pure. Verse 2 points to the celebration phase, revealing that when Christ returns, we will be like Him and we will see Him as He is.

What a marvelous truth! When the bridegroom returns for His bride, He will remove her remaining sin, making her forever perfect as He is perfect. Remember *nasa,* the Hebrew verb derived from *nissun* which is the word used for the celebration phase? Well, *nasa* is not only translated as "to lift up." It can also be translated as "forgive or accept."[11]

Nasa is also sometimes translated exalt or honor in the Old Testament (see Num. 14:19; Mic. 1:8). The Hebrew root word for the final phase of the Jewish marriage process signifies the taking away of sin. Don't you love the consistency of God's Word?

Compare 1 Corinthians 15:51-52 and Philippians 3:20-21.
Mark each statement below true (*T*) or false (*F*).
- _T_ All believers will be changed in an instant.
- _F_ Believers will be allowed to choose their glorified bodies.
- _T_ Jesus will complete our transformation.
- _T_ All believers will receive glorified bodies.
- _F_ Our citizenship will remain on earth.

Discover the Meaning

When Christ appears we will see Him as He is and we will be like Him (1 John 3:2). A perfect match made in heaven! Let's stop for a moment and allow this astounding truth to sink in. When Christ returns to claim His bride, we will see Him in all His glory—just as He is.

Notice the connection between seeing Jesus as He really is and being like Him. In this life, sin blinds us from fully seeing Him. We see Him as a poor reflection in an antique mirror, but not fully (1 Cor. 13:12). The more we see Jesus as He is, the more intimately we know Him and become like Him. When Jesus returns, we'll see and understand Him clearly because the barrier of sin will be completely removed, and we will be forever changed. The bride's perfection will finally and forever match that of her glorious bridegroom. Then we will experience spiritual intimacy beyond imagination and eternal joy beyond compare.

Make It Personal

I can't close today's look at the divine love story without mentioning another beautiful aspect of the Jewish marriage experience. To the ancient Hebrew, marriage was often represented by the bridegroom's covering the bride with his cloak (see Ezek. 16:8; Ruth 3:9). Spreading a covering or tent over the bride represented acceptance and protection. This symbolic gesture became an important part of the Jewish marriage celebration that endures today. The Jewish bride and groom often sit together under a tent or canopy during the wedding celebration. This wedding canopy, known as a *huppah,* symbolized the couple's new life together.

Read Revelation 7:15-17. How does what we've just learned enhance your understanding of the passage?

God's Protection, comfort + love
He Who sits on the throne will spread His tabernacle over them

The perfect union of Christ and His bride is a defining moment in God's eternal plan, the fulfillment of one of the most exciting events on the kingdom calendar. "Covering" signifies marriage. This passage gives insight into what eternity with Christ will be like. The old will pass away and the bride will enjoy a whole new aspect of relationship with her beloved. She will be at His side forever. He will be her shelter, protecting her from hunger, thirst, heat, and the elements. He will guide her to springs of living water and wipe every tear from her eyes (Rev. 7:17).

I have often tried to imagine this glorious new life. What will it be like to continually dwell in the presence of God where there is fullness of joy? How will I respond to such total protection? To such comfort? To such love?

What do you find most significant about our glimpse into the new life that awaits us?

that my transformation will be completed + there will be no more sin

How can we balance waiting for God to complete the transformation and preparing for Christ's return?

Live what I believe, Focus on the reality of His return. Actively prepare + be ready for His return

Dear friends, Christ *will* return and we will be forever changed! Do you believe it? Do you live it? Writing this study has continually reminded me of the importance of my attitude about the return of Christ. I must confess, the reality of His return had become lost in the shuffle of my busy life. Renewing my focus on the certainty of His return and the truth of what it means for those who believe has given me a greater sense of purpose. I truly desire to do all I can to actively prepare for His coming … to be found ready when the bridegroom appears.

Day Five
Until Then

We have followed many paths in our quest to understand how Jewish wedding imagery illustrates our relationship with Christ. Together we've traveled the pages of Scripture, discovering fascinating wedding customs, learning the importance of this time on God's kingdom calendar, finding greater insight into our personal responsibilities, experiencing the value of community, hearing vital messages from the divine bridegroom, and encountering afresh the excitement of His return. I hope all we've explored means as much to you as it does to me. I'm encouraged to know that although our time together will soon end, we'll each continue in our collective duty to attend the bride. And if we never have a chance to meet on earth, I'm confident we will joyfully greet each other in the coming divine celebration!

More than anything, I want these truths to make a lasting difference: to motivate us to continue learning and allowing God to transform us. I've participated in some wonderful Bible studies that made no real difference in my life. The materials were not at fault. The problem was me; I failed to allow God to change my life.

Can you recall a time when a study of God's Word truly moved you, yet you experienced no lasting change? If so, explain.

_____

Search the Scripture

In preparing to part company, I'd like for us to focus on what happens when the study concludes and life resumes. I believe what we do next will be the greatest measure of the value of our time together. Let's allow God as much room as possible to prepare us for the next step in our spiritual transformation.

What does Hebrews 2:1 encourage us to do?

Pay Closer attention to what we have heard,

Why?

So that we do not drift away from it

What did the author of Hebrews mean by "pay more careful attention"?

❍ He meant we should listen more closely to the Bible's teaching.
❍ He meant we should develop a better memory for Bible facts.
◉ He meant we should incorporate biblical teaching into our daily lives.
❍ He meant that we should take notes on Bible teaching.

Some believers in Ephesus failed to adjust their daily lives to Paul's teaching. They received Christ but continued to sin without giving thought to the consequences.

According to Ephesians 4:17-19, what are some of the results of failing to incorporate God's Word into our daily lives? (Check all that apply.)

◉ We become spiritually ignorant.
❍ Our thinking becomes futile.
◉ We become separated from the life God has for us.
❍ Our sins increase.

Like me, you may wonder how you can pay careful attention to all we've learned about God and our relationship with Him over these past weeks. After all, I can hardly remember when it's my turn to work in the nursery, bake a cake for the fellowship dinner, or host the youth group breakfast. I don't, however, believe the author of Hebrews used the phrase "pay more careful attention" merely to encourage us to sharpen our memories. Don't forget, the Holy Spirit living in us faithfully reminds us of what we've heard just when we need it (John 14:26). The question each of us must ask is, *Am I paying careful attention to what I'm learning about Scripture by treasuring and living it—allowing it to transform all areas of my life?* or *Am I only growing in my knowledge of God's Word?*

The Hebrews passage suggests we don't pay enough attention to the spiritual truths we've been taught. That attention deficit can have devastating results. When we don't pay careful attention to the Spirit's reminders of truths we've learned, allowing Him to incorporate them into our lives, we drift away from those truths and cannot fulfill our God-given purposes—including our duty to attend the bride. For any Bible study to produce lasting change, we must become better listeners, carefully paying attention and responding when the Spirit speaks. In short, we must become spiritually mature.

Discover the Meaning

We've learned that believers are called to attend the bride with steadfast devotion through spiritual maturity (transformation). That sounds easy enough, but in reality, preparing for the bridegroom's return is a supernatural challenge. Difficulties and distractions seem to increase as the time of His return draws nearer. The process of personal spiritual maturity can be slow and frustrating, but with the Holy Spirit's guidance we can withstand the challenges. Hebrews 10:19-25 tells us how.

- Listen to praise music.
- Write a love song to God.
- Make a list of ways God has blessed you.
- Share what God is doing in your life with a friend.
- Read a devotional book.
- Journal your prayer requests and God's responses.
- Write a letter expressing your love for Him.
- Fellowship with other believers.
- Study the Bible.
- Sing a praise.
- Pray alone.
- Pray with a friend.

Underline the key "let us" statements.

Therefore, brothers, since we have confidence to enter the Most Holy Place by the blood of Jesus, by a new and living way opened for us through the curtain, that is, his body, and since we have a great priest over the house of God, <u>let us draw near to God with a sincere heart in full assurance of faith, having our hearts sprinkled to cleanse us from a guilty conscience and having our bodies washed with pure water.</u> <u>Let us hold unswervingly to the hope we profess,</u> for he who promised is faithful. And <u>let us consider how we may spur one another on toward love and good deeds.</u> <u>Let us not give up meeting together,</u> as some are in the habit of doing, but <u>let us encourage one another</u>—and all the more as you see the Day approaching.

This passage sums up much of what we've learned together during our study. <u>It also encourages us</u> as we, with God's help, strive to live what we've learned. As we've discovered, the divine bridegroom lovingly provides all we need to faithfully persevere through hardships and to spiritually grow as we prepare for His return. Our relationship with Him has opened a new and living way for us, a way that brings certain victory. No circumstance is too difficult for Him—we can be faithful because He is faithful! Let's consider how we can faithfully persevere in the days ahead.

1. *"Let us draw near to God."*
   How can we draw near to God? *Trusting Him - Intimate relationship w/ Him*
   Relying on God & remaining in Him

Beloved, we serve a God who graciously invites us to get closer to Him. Our personal friendship with the divine bridegroom has opened the way for us to come nearer to God the Father. We must boldly take advantage of this miraculous access by relying on God and remaining in Him. Drawing near to God is not only an amazing privilege, it is an absolute necessity. Preparing for Christ's return requires intimate relationship with God. He lovingly implores us to come closer.

   On a scale of 1 (far from God) to 10 (very near God), how would you rate your closeness to God right now?

   In the margin are a few things you can try to grow closer in your relationship with the Lord. Underline your favorites, and commit to doing them this week.

2. *"Let us hold unswervingly to the hope we profess."*
   What "hope" do we as believers profess? (See day 5 of week 3.)
   Jesus's certain Return. He promised He would
   Jesus to Coming return

Why should we hold to this hope (Heb. 10:23)? ————————→ *Christ*

Because He promised and He Is faithful

We know that attending Christ's bride in preparation for the bridegroom's return can sometimes be discouraging. Therefore, neglecting to hold onto Christ's promise to return becomes a very real hazard for many Christians. During times of frustration, it's important that we hold steadfastly to the hope we have in Christ's certain return. We are His bride, purchased by His love. When we fix our hope on Him and rely on His faithfulness, He will not disappoint us.

What can you do today to tighten your grip on your hope in Christ?

_____

Write Philippians 3:14 on a card. Carry it with you wherever you go. Let the words inspire and encourage you in the days ahead.

I press on toward the goal for the prize of the upward call of God in Christ Jesus.

3. "Let us spur one another on toward good deeds."
How can you spur someone on toward good deeds?

_____

Why is it so important that you do?

_____

Throughout our study we've seen that attending Christ's bride is the responsibility of all believers. By God's design, we need to work with others to accomplish His purposes. He works through our relationships, providing us with the love, encouragement, and the accountability we need. We can measure our progress in the preparation process by evaluating our ability to help, to encourage, and to work with one another.

How have you benefitted from other believers' encouragements? *Yes*

Before, During & after Richard's heart surgery in June 2010 + his arm & eye melanoma surgeries + treatments in 2011
GCBS They prayed over me + lifted me & Richard to the Lord & gave me peace

In the margin, write the names of at least three believers whom you can spur on toward good deeds this week. Make plans to write, call, or speak with each one. Remind them of God's love and encourage them to keep working for Him.

4. "Let us not give up meeting together."
What are the benefits of regularly meeting with other believers?
(See day 4 of week 4.)

fellowship by spending time with, caring for, and sharing w/ one another

Christ's impending return is our greatest motivation to gather together. Preparing the bride's beautiful ornaments of God's grace requires that we meet regularly. Gathering together to worship God, receive instruction, fellowship with one another, and evangelize further prepares the bride for His return. The less we gather, the fewer opportunities we have to complete preparations for the bridegroom's glorious coming. By working together in God's power, we are better able to comprehend the love of Christ and do what He has called us to do (see Eph. 3:16-19).

Describe your own faithfulness in meeting together with other believers.

every Monday night

How might your absence impact those who regularly gather?

My insights on the Precepts Study
The Ladies @ Laurel Creek seem to Look for me
to arrive

Perhaps the most significant truth God taught me through this study can be summed up in four words: *what we do matters.* The Father's plan, our close friendship with the bridegroom, our place as a part of the bride, our personal call to attend the bride and prepare for Christ's return—*they all count on an eternal scale!* Now that I recognize this fact, I'm no longer content to passively wait for Christ to return; I'm compelled to diligently prepare.

Why should we persevere through indescribable difficulties? Because everything we've been called to do is critical to preparing the bride. Christ will return, and we—His love and His bride—must be ready.

Make It Personal

I once heard someone say, "The two greatest things about God are that He loves us where we are, but does not want us to stay there"; this truth has become the heart of my life and ministry. Throughout this study my greatest desire has been to help us better understand our call to diligently prepare for Christ's return by staying actively engaged in the divine process of continuous transformation. You see, Beloved, attending the bride is not about what we can do for God, but what God can do for us. While our personal journeys may each be unique, we are all moving toward the same glorious destination.

Our personal transformation is a part of the broader transformation of Christ's bride. As we allow our lives to be transformed by God and join fellow believers in the preparation of the bride's beautiful ornaments of grace, we become a catalyst for change in others. In 1 Timothy 4:15 Paul sums it up, "Be diligent in these matters; give yourself wholly to them, so that everyone may see your progress."

I pray this study has helped you see church differently and that you will act accordingly. I've discovered that effective learning is not complete until action is taken based on the new understanding. It does not, however, end there. We must each remain open to new insights and understanding that produce further changes

Perhaps the most significant truth God taught me through this study can be summed up in four words: *what we do matters.*

so that the divine process of our transformation into the perfected bride of Christ can continue.

When you turn the final page of this study, will your life be any different than when we began? Will you be further transformed or just more knowledgeable?

Please open the personal evaluation you completed at the beginning of week 1 and review your responses. Consider what God has revealed to you during this study. How have your views changed?

_____

How will you use this new perspective?

_____

Will you join me in committing to invest our lives in things that really matter?

If you will, pray with me now:

Heavenly Father, we acknowledge that You alone are God and we praise Your holy name. We thank you for loving us enough to appoint our lives with divine purpose. Thank you for offering us friendship with the bridegroom and allowing us to become a part of the bride of Christ. We gratefully accept the honor of serving Christ and attending His bride. We acknowledge that only You can transform us and we commit ourselves to Your divine will. Teach us to be women who are continually open and ready to be transformed. Help us to live daily in the truth of Christ's imminent return. Intensify our longing for Christ's glorious appearing and help us keep the joy of that moment always before us in the challenging days ahead.

In the precious name of Jesus, Amen.

"Now to him who is able to do immeasurably more than all we ask or imagine, according to his power that is at work within us, to him be glory in the church and in Christ Jesus throughout all generations, for ever and ever! Amen" (Eph. 3:20-21).

I want you to know what an incredible privilege it's been to share these weeks with you! Our time together has been invaluable to my relationship with the bridegroom, His Father, His church, and my fellow attendants. I pray it's been the same for you.

I hope to see you soon ... either here, or at the wedding celebration!

You are dearly loved!

Martha

Endnotes

Session 1

1. Alfred J. Kolatch, *The Jewish Book of Why* (Middle Village, NY: Jonathan David Publishers, Inc., 1981), 27.
2. George Robinson, *Essential Judaism* (New York: Pocket Books, 2000), 160.
3. Ibid.
4. Mendell Lewittes, *A Survey of Jewish Marriage* (Northvale, NJ: Jason Aronson, Inc., 1994), 31.
5. Barney Kasdan, *God's Appointed Customs* (Baltimore: Lederer Books, 1996), 48.
6. Ibid., 50.
7. Ibid., 60.
8. Ibid., 51.
9. Lewittes, 86.
10. Os Guinness, *The Call* (Nashville: Word Publishers, 1998), 101.
11. Robinson, 160.
12. Paul P. Enns, *Shepherd's Notes-Manners and Customs of Bible Times* (Nashville: Broadman and Holman Publishers, 2000), 28.
13. Wayne Dosick, *Living Judaism: The Complete Guide to Jewish Belief, Tradition, and Practice* (New York: Harper Collins Publishers, Inc., 1995), 298.
14. Lewittes, 35.
15. Ibid.

Session 2

1. Barney Kasdan, *God's Appointed Customs* (Baltimore: Lederer Books, 1996), 49.
2. Michael L. Sotlow, *Jewish Marriage in Antiquity* (Princeton, NJ: Princeton University Press, 2001), 163.
3. Wayne Dosick, *Living Judaism: The Complete Guide to Jewish Belief, Tradition, and Practice* (New York: Harper Collins Publishers, Inc., 1995), 296.
4. Paul P. Enns, *Shepherd's Notes-Manners and Customs of Bible Times* (Nashville: Broadman and Holman Publishers, 2000), 29.
5. Mendell Lewittes, *A Survey of Jewish Marriage* (Northvale, NJ: Jason Aronson, Inc., 1994), 70.
6. Kasdan, 60.
7. Ibid., 52.
8. George Robinson, *Essential Judaism* (New York: Pocket Books, 2000), 160.
9. Ibid., 161.
10. Ibid., 161.
11. Dosick, 298.
12. Lewittes, 72.
13. W.E. Vine, *Vine's Complete Expository Dictionary* (Nashville: Thomas Nelson, Inc., Publishers, 1985), 135.

14. David C. Gross, *Under the Wedding Canopy* (New York: Hippocrene Books, 1996), 50.
15. Ibid.
16. Kasdan, 51.
17. Ibid.
18. Ibid.
19. Ibid.
20. Dosick, 296.

Session 3

1. Barney Kasdan, *God's Appointed Customs* (Baltimore: Lederer Books, 1996), 51.
2. "Jewish Wedding" Retrieved from *http://www.ahavat-israel.com/ahavat/torat/marriage.asp* Oct. 6, 2004.
3. W.E. Vine, *An Expository Dictionary of New Testament Words* (Nashville: Thomas Nelson, Inc., Publishers, 1984), 44.
4. *Hebrew Greek Key Word Study Bible.* (Grand Rapids: AMG International, Inc., 1996), 1641.
5. Ibid.
6. Ibid.
7. Vine, 268.
8. Warren W. Wiersbe, *The Bible Exposition Commentary,* New Testament, Vol. 2 (Colorado Springs: Cook Communication Ministries, 2001), 51.

Session 4

1. Joseph H. Thayer, *Thayer's Greek-English Lexicon of the New Testament* (Peabody, MA: Hendrickson Publishers, Inc., 2002), 856.
2. *Webster's World Encyclopedia 2001* (Brookvale, Australia: Webster World Pty. Ltd., 2000) electronic ed.
3. Merrill F. Unger and William White, Jr. eds., *Nelson's Expository Dictionary of the Old Testament.* (Nashville: Thomas Nelson, Inc., Publishers, 1984), 123.
4. Thayer, 473.
5. *Nelson's Expository Dictionary of the Old Testament,* 123.
6. Carolyn Curtis, ed., "Straying from the truth of the gospel" *On Mission,* Special Issue 2003, 9.
7. Thayer, 352.
8. Ibid., 599.
9. *Hebrew Greek Key Word Study Bible.* (AMG International, Inc., 1996), 1641.
10. Ibid.

Session 5

1. *Hebrew Greek Key Word Study Bible.* (Grand Rapids: AMG International, Inc., 1996), n.p.
2. W.E. Vine, *An Expository Dictionary of New Testament Words* (Nashville: Thomas Nelson, Inc., Publishers, 1985), 44.
3. Warren E. Wiersbe, *The Bible Exposition Commentary,* New Testament Vol. 1 (Colorado Springs: Cook Communications Ministries, 2001), 59.
4. Ibid.
5. Ibid., 573.
6. Retrieved from *http://www.studylight.org/com/jfb/view.cgi?book=re&chapter=002.* Apr. 27, 2005.
7. Wiersbe, Vol. 2, 578.
8. Ibid., 575.
9. Ibid.
10. Ibid., 573.
11. Ibid., 574.
12. Ibid., 579.
13. Ibid.

Session 6

1. Barney Kasdan, *God's Appointed Customs* (Baltimore: Lederer Books, 1996), 51.
2. *Hebrew Greek Key Word Study Bible* (Grand Rapids: AMG International, Inc., 1996.), n.p.
3. *The Brown-Driver-Briggs Hebrew and English Lexicon.* (Boston: Houghton, Mifflin and Company, 1906), 670.
4. Kasdan, 51.
5. Paul P. Enns, *Shepherd's Notes: Manners and Customs in Bible Times* (Nashville: Broadman and Holman Publishers, 2000), 30.
6. Kasdan, 51.
7. Ibid., 51.
8. W.E. Vine, *An Expository Dictionary of New Testament Words* (Nashville: Thomas Nelson, Inc., Publishers, 1994), 519.
9. *Hebrew Greek Key Word Study Bible,* 1570.
10. *Halley's Bible Handbook* (Grand Rapids: Zondervan, 2000), 958.
12. *Hebrew Greek Key Word Study Bible,* 1981.

Leader Guide

1. W. Phillip Keller, *A Shepherd Looks at Psalm 23* (Grand Rapids: Zondervan, 1970), 80.
2. David C. Gross, *Under the Wedding Canopy, Love and Marriage in Judaism* (New York: Hippocrene Books, 1996), 45.

Leader Guide

Thank you for choosing to facilitate a study of *Attending the Bride of Christ.* I'm so honored to partner with you on this journey, and I pray God will richly bless your sacrificial service to Christ's bride.

Are you considering conducting a retreat either to launch this study or to celebrate its conclusion? If so, visit www.lifeway.com/women to find helpful suggestions and downloadable resources. Additional ideas can also be found at www.attendingthebride.com.

Attending the Bride of Christ: Preparing for His Return is designed for study in small home groups, Bible study groups, and accountability groups. This leader guide is designed to help you facilitate 6 group sessions plus an optional introductory session in any of these settings. Because this is an in-depth study, some groups may choose to take a longer time for the study. Follow the Holy Spirit's leading about taking more than one week to complete some of the subjects. You do not have to be locked into the six-week format.

I strongly recommend that you include the introductory session because it provides time to distribute books and get acquainted; however, if you choose not to have an introduction, make sure each participant receives her workbook in plenty of time to complete week 1 before your first meeting. The participants' completion of each week's material is vital to the quality of the small group members' discussion.

Don't feel you must cover every activity in the leader guide. It contains more discussion topics and activities than you will have time to cover in your weekly sessions. Be flexible and consider the unique needs of your group as you prepare. Keep in mind that our goal is furthering each individual's process of spiritual transformation. Look for opportunities to challenge group participants to allow God to use new insights to change their actions. Most importantly, allow the Holy Spirit to direct your group's time together.

It's important for you, as the group's facilitator, to complete each week's assignments before group time. Highlight facts and verses within the weekly material that you find especially touching or valuable so you'll be better prepared to share your own insights with the group. Always seek how God wants you to apply His Word. Make sure to spend time each week praying for participants. Encourage them throughout the study and quickly contact anyone who misses a session. Make it your goal to build up your sisters in Christ as you work and learn together.

God bless you as you shepherd the small group He has so graciously given you, and know that I am praying for you as you personally attend the bride!

Getting Started

1. If you plan to conduct *Attending the Bride of Christ* in your local church, enlist the support of your pastor.
2. Select the dates and times during which your group can meet. If you are meeting during the day, you may want to offer childcare.
3. One month prior to your first intended meeting date, send out invitations that include the study's name, meeting times, location, and RSVP information to the ladies of your church or to those who may want to participate in a home study.
4. After determining how may participants you'll have, obtain a copy of the *Attending the Bride of Christ* workbook for each.

Introductory Session (Optional)
Before the Session

1. Familiarize yourself with the *Attending the Bride of Christ* member book.
   • Read the Introduction to and day 1 of week 1.
   • Review the Table of Contents for an overview of the study.
   • Examine the Kingdom Calendar illustration provided on page 153 of the leader guide.
2. Prepare a participant attendance sheet. At the top of the sheet, briefly explain that the information will be shared with group members so they can contact one another and will be kept within the group. Allow space for their names, addresses, phone numbers, and e-mail addresses. List your personal information on the first line.
3. Gather markers, pens, name tags, and a basket for collecting workbook money.

4. Pray for each participant, asking God to use this study to help the ladies have a clear understanding of His plan and their part in it. Pray that participants will allow God to use this time to continue the process of their personal spiritual transformation and that this study will encourage them to more actively serve Christ's bride.

5. Plan to arrive to your classroom early. You'll want to arrange the room in a comfortable circle that enhances group interaction and sharing.

6. Write the word *church* across a tear sheet with a marker or on a chalkboard. On a piece of scrap paper, jot down your personal definition of church and where you developed that understanding.

During the Session (1 hour)

1. Greet participants as they arrive. Invite them to sign the attendance sheet and prepare their name tags.

2. Try your best to begin on time. Opening in prayer will get the class time off to a strong start.

3. Introduce yourself and give a brief explanation of why you chose to participate in this particular study. Ask group participants to do the same.

4. Distribute participants' workbooks. If your church prefers individuals pay for their workbooks, invite individuals to leave payment in the basket as you dismiss.

5. Explain that your group time will be based largely on open discussion. Encourage participants to share their insights with the group and remind them that the completion of their weekly homework will contribute to the quality of the group time. Explain, however, that participants should still attend group sessions even if they are unable to finish their home assignments.

6. Ask for agreement that everything discussed in your group will remain confidential.

7. Briefly introduce the study through these activities:
   a. Call attention to the word c*hurch* written on the board or tear sheet. Ask participants what immediately comes to mind when they hear the word *church*. If they are hesitant to share, offer the responses you wrote prior to group time. List group responses on the board or tear sheet. Follow up by asking participants where we get our ideas or understanding about church.
   b. Ask, What is the purpose of church? After giving a few moments for response, explain that *Attend-*

ing the Bride of Christ seeks to help readers better understand the church's true identity and purpose as well as this time on the kingdom calendar. Point out that the church is the bride of Christ and she has been called to prepare for His return by joining God in completing the assignments He gave her. Challenge participants to look for clues into God's purpose for the church and each believer's role in that purpose as they begin to work on week 1. Encourage them to highlight or underline insights and clues they discover as they work.

   c. Point out that the study will explore the significance of the marriage imagery Scripture uses to describe Christ's relationship with the church. Explain that the study is for anyone who desires to learn more about the relationship between Christ and His followers. Emphasize the fact that participants do not need to have a personal marriage experience to fully participate in the study.

   d. Explain that the study is designed to teach believers to discover new meaning in familiar Scriptures by introducing them to historical facts and often missed biblical details. Ask a volunteer to read the 23rd Psalm out loud. Then read to the group the following passage from Phillip Keller's, *A Shepherd Looks at Psalm 23:*

> "Another interesting use of the rod in the Shepherd's hand was to examine and count the sheep. In the terminology of the Old Testament this was referred to as passing "under the rod" (Ezek. 20:37). This meant not only coming under the owner's control and authority, but also to be subject to his most careful, intimate and firsthand examination. A sheep that passed "under the rod" was one that had been counted and looked over with great care to make sure all was well with it."[1]

Reread the verse from Psalm 23:4 to the group. Invite participants to share how this historical information about shepherding might enhance understanding of Psalm 23:4. For example, the comfort of the shepherd's rod means more than protection; it also represents personal attention, care, and intimate relationship. Explain that during the study you will seek to enrich your understanding of the Jewish marriage imagery used in Scripture by learning more about ancient Jewish wedding customs.

e. Encourage participants to share about times when learning about biblical history or Jewish culture enhanced their understanding of Scripture.

f. Briefly review the organization of the study. Ask participants to look over the daily assignments for week 1. Encourage them to complete each week's study prior to the weekly meetings. Point out that each daily assignment should take between 30 and 45 minutes to complete.

8. Remind participants of the meeting times for each session. Encourage timeliness and attendance. Emphasize the importance of both individual study and group participation. Ask them to bring their workbooks and Bibles to every meeting.

9. If time allows, divide participants into groups of two or three. Invite each to share with her small group one prayer concern she has as she begins this new journey. Ask each group to spend time in prayer for one another throughout the week.

10. Close by praying that God will grant participants open and teachable hearts as they begin this quest to grow in understanding His purpose for the church—Christ's bride—and for themselves as believers.

11. Express your desire to minister to each woman personally during this study. Point out that your personal contact information is at the top of the attendance sheet, then verbally offer your phone number to the group. Encourage them to call you this week with any questions, concerns, or prayer requests.

After the Session

1. Take a few moments to reflect on this session. Consider what spiritual or mental preparations you need to make for the next one. Make notes on the introduction page of week 1.

2. Record unique reasons participants gave for taking the study. (Keep these in a safe place for review during our last session.)

3. Note any information or impressions that will help you in praying specifically for each participant throughout the week.

4. Secure any additional workbooks needed. Try to deliver them quickly so that participants will have plenty of time to complete their home assignments.

5. If time allows, send out thank you e-mails or quick notes to those who provided their addresses. Tell them you are excited to have them in the group and hope they'll be blessed and encouraged by the study.

Session One: A Picture of Relationship
Before the Session

1. If you did not have an introductory session, please follow the Getting Started and *Before the Session* suggestions on page 141.

2. Make sure all group participants receive their books at least one week prior to group session 1.

3. Obtain enough three-by-five-inch cards and pens so that each participant will have one.

4. Complete week 1's material. Highlight facts and insights that are especially meaningful to you. Be prepared to share your favorites with the group.

5. When you complete your week 1 homework, read the list of discussion starters offered for this week's group session. Since you will not have time to do all of the suggested options, go ahead and circle two to four that your group might find especially interesting.

6. If you select option 4-f, you'll need to ask one participant to briefly share with the group the story of when she accepted God's offer of personal relationship. Ask her to plan to speak for 1–2 minutes.

7. Pray for each participant. Thank God for bringing each one into your group, and ask the Lord to give them divine guidance as they dedicate time to completing their homework assignments. Pray that God will reveal more of Himself and His plan to each woman as she spends time with Him.

8. Arrive early for your session so you'll have plenty of time to arrange and prepare the classroom.

During the Session (1 hour)

1. Welcome participants as they arrive. If this is your first session together, provide an attendance sheet, name tags, and pens at the door.

2. Promptly begin in prayer, thanking God that He has an eternal plan and that each believer is invited to be a part of it.

3. Explain that each week the group will discuss material participants have studied individually during the week. Encourage them to complete each learning activity to get the most out of their study.

4. Begin discussion with some of these starters:

   a. Invite a volunteer to read Revelation 19:6-9, which describes the scene of the divine wedding feast. Ask participants to share whether or not they believe this passage describes a true event. Follow up by inviting participants to explain how focusing on the future might help us better understand the present.

b. Ask these questions: What does it mean that the Bible is the final authority? Why is it important to recognize the superiority of Scripture? After giving members time for discussion, affirm that the Bible is God's Word and truth. Ask a volunteer to read aloud 2 Timothy 3:16. Suggest that participants highlight the passage in their Bibles.

c. Involve participants in a discussion of the significance of Jesus' identity as the divine bridegroom. Ask them if the role changed their perception of Him. If so, how?

d. Ask a volunteer to read the three important ways Jesus demonstrated His friendship with us (see p. 16). Ask them to explain how they reciprocate Jesus' offer of friendship.

e. Ask participants, What are the different roles we as believers have in Christ? Write them on a poster or tear sheet. Encourage participants to share which spiritual role they struggle with most and why.

f. Remind participants of the ancient Jewish bride's right to accept or reject the offer of relationship. Have the participant you contacted prior to meeting tell the group her story of accepting God's offer of personal relationship. Ask if anyone accepted God's offer of salvation during this week's study. If so, take a few moments to rejoice over the life-changing decision! Welcome her as a new and important part of the bride of Christ. Stop and pray for the new attendant as she begins her journey of personal transformation. Thank God for His abundant grace and mercy.

5. Have a volunteer explain the significance of the bride price (pp. 20-21). Write "The Price He Paid" on a poster or marker board. Ask, What price did Christ pay for His bride? Ask participants to explain how the knowledge that Christ paid such a price for them as individuals made them feel.

6. Ask participants to list ways God has demonstrated how much He values the church. (Examples include: He gave His Son for her; He gave her the Holy Spirit; He gave her spiritual gifts; He is transforming her into Christ's bride). Write their responses on a poster or tear sheet. Then hand out three-by-five-inch cards. Encourage participants to think about their own attitudes and actions toward the church as they look at the list of ways God demonstrates the church's value. Invite participants to write on their cards one-sentence, confidential summaries of how they generally respond to Christ's bride. Then ask them to brainstorm ways they can apply the value God gives the church to their own perceptions of her. Ask them why it's important that they do. Challenge participants to daily seek God's help in seeing the church as He sees her and acting accordingly.

7. Ask participants to share insights from this week's study that they found particularly relevant or touching. (You may want to share your thoughts to get things started.) Ask those sharing what their new insights might prompt them to do differently.

8. Close with prayer, thanking God for each participant by name.

9. Challenge participants to complete the homework for week 2 before the next group meeting. Encourage those members who may have fallen behind to catch up with the assignments.

After the Session
1. Take time to reflect on the session. Ask yourself:
   • How well did I begin and end on time?
   • Whom do I need to encourage to participate?
   • What can I do to get everyone involved?
   • What specific needs were mentioned that I can pray for this week?
   Record your thoughts on page 28.
2. Contact participants who are falling behind on homework or attendance. Don't scold. Offer encouragement. Be willing to be a listening ear and always ask if they have any specific requests for which you can pray.

Session Two: Past Reflections of the Future
Before the Session
1. Complete the week 2 material. Highlight facts and insights that are especially meaningful to you. Be prepared to share your favorites with the group.
2. When you complete week 2 homework, read through the list of discussion starters offered for this week's group session. Since you will not have time to do all of the suggested options, follow the Holy Spirit's

guidance and go ahead and circle 2 to 4 that you think your group might find especially valuable.

3. Pray for each participant. Ask God to help them set aside time to study His Word. Ask Him to provide divine insight and encouragement to all the women throughout the week.

4. Select CDs or tapes of praise music or arrange for someone to provide accompaniment. If you choose to use a CD or tape, don't forget your CD or tape player. Consider songs about Christ's sacrificial love like "How Beautiful"[Is the Body of Christ], "In Remembrance of Me," "Above All," "Are You Washed in the Blood."

5. Obtain two posters or tear sheets and markers.

6. Prepare your room and arrive early for the session.

During the Session (1 hour)

1. Welcome participants as they arrive.

2. Making certain to start on time, begin the session with praise and worship. Depending on your group's dynamic, sing or listen to songs that focus on Christ's example of love and sacrifice.

3. Ask a volunteer to read 1 Thessalonians 5:23-24. Pray, thanking God for providing the way for believers to remain set apart and holy. Acknowledge that it's only by His great faithfulness and power that we can be kept blameless at Christ's return.

4. Begin with some of these discussion starters:

   a. Ask a volunteer to share her own betrothal or engagement story. Then ask volunteers to share their reactions to the evidence of the divine betrothal presented in the lesson. Point out that the first two weeks of study have been filled with exciting ancient wedding imagery. Invite participants to share which of the ancient imagery facts they have found most fascinating and why.

   b. Invite a volunteer to share the significance of the comparison of the Bible with the Jewish *ketubah*. Ask how believers can demonstrate their appreciation and reverence for Scripture. Ask participants to brainstorm ways a church demonstrates how much it values God's Word.

   c. Invite participants to share examples of how they have found hope in Scripture (p. 36). Ask, How did that hope encourage you or change your thinking toward your situation?

   d. Read Luke 10:25-27, the parable of the good Samaritan. Ask participants to explain how

believers and the church can remain set apart yet still touch the world for Christ. Ask them to share personal examples of how they touch the world for Him.

   e. Encourage members to explain the difference between waiting for and preparing for the return of Christ. List action words that could be used to describe preparation. Ask participants how believers can move from simply waiting for Christ's return to actively preparing.

   f. Ask a volunteer to explain the connection between Jesus' mercy in not wanting anyone to perish and His desire to be united with His bride (p. 43) Invite participants to share how this connection has affected their perspectives on sharing Christ with the lost. Ask how what they've learned will change their future actions.

5. Invite participants to share their most significant insight from this week's study. If necessary, share your thoughts to get things started. Encourage them to consider how this new insight will change their actions.

6. Divide participants into two groups. Give each group a poster or tear sheet. Ask one group to review Galatians 5:16-18, 22-25 and Romans 8:5-9 then symbolically portray through pictures what it means to be filled with and live by the Spirit. Ask the other group to read Colossians 3:1-10 and 1 Peter 1:13-16 then symbolically portray through pictures what it means to be and remain set apart for Christ. After allowing 3–5 minutes work time, ask each group to explain their drawing to the class.

7. Have a volunteer read Acts 9:31. Explain that you'd like the groups to spend time praying for the church. Suggest they begin by praying this Scripture (That the church would be strengthened and encouraged by the Holy Spirit and that the church would grow in numbers and live in the fear of the Lord). Then each person within each group should pray for your pastor, other church leaders, and members. Ask God to speak clearly and to remove any obstacles to the work of the Spirit from among you.

8. Close in prayer. Thank God for what He has done for the church. Ask Him to help us see her as He sees her and to have the same attitude toward her as He does.

9. Challenge participants to complete week 3's homework before the next session.

After the Session

Take a few moments to reflect on this session. Consider which participants most need a phone call or card of encouragement this week. Make a note of their names and when you plan to contact them.

Session Three: The Divine Partnership

Before the Session

1. Complete week 3's material. Highlight facts and insights that are especially meaningful to you. Be prepared to share your favorites with the group.

2. Read through the discussion starters offered for this week's group session. Since you will not have time to do all of the suggested options, circle 2 to 4 that you think your group might find especially interesting.

3. See number 4 under this week's "During the Session" heading. Considering the interests of your group, pre-select a service project to be presented at this week's group meeting and completed during the next. Ideas include, but are not limited to, asking participants to bring benevolence items to support one of your church's ministries or asking them to stay after meeting to tidy the church building.

4. Spend time in prayer. Ask God to prepare individual participants for the group session. Pray that He will reveal the often unseen work on the Holy Spirit among the group. Ask Him to help everyone stay committed to the journey and to prepare each heart to receive a very personal message through this week's study.

5. Obtain blank sheets of colored paper and pens for each participant.

6. Provide lemonade or coffee, paper cups, plates, napkins, and cookies for all.

7. If time allows, send e-mails or notes of encouragement to group members, reminding them of this week's meeting and telling them how much you appreciate their faithfulness.

8. Arrive early and prepare your room for the small-group session.

During the Session (1 hour)

1. Welcome participants as they arrive, offering them something to drink and a cookie. It's important that they see you serving them.

2. Invite participants to share ways they were personally challenged in their relationship with the church this week. Pray aloud for the group that God will continue to stretch and help each person grow in her relationships with Him and His church.

3. Begin with several of these discussion starters:

   a. Read 1 Peter 4:10-11. Ask the group to list the facts about service these verses give. As a group, form a one-sentence definition of *service*.

   b. Write the word *devoted* on the board or tear sheet. Pass out sheets of colored paper and pens. Ask each participant to make a simple drawing that expresses what *"devoted"* means. After they have completed the drawings, give volunteers a chance to explain their pictures to the group. Then invite participants to discuss what it means to be steadfastly devoted to the church. Ask how this new understanding will change their actions.

   c. Have a volunteer explain the importance of having an accurate measure of our readiness (see p. 54). Then ask a volunteer to explain why spiritual maturity is essential to attending the bride with steadfast devotion.

   d. Remind the group of the Jewish tradition of community involvement in the preparation for the wedding celebration. Invite them to compare this to the believer's relationship with the church. Guide them to consider the significance of God's plan that all believers be actively involved in preparing for Christ's return. Ask:

      1) What things is our church currently doing (or could do) to keep more participants involved?

      2) How can we as believers more effectively communicate to inactive participants that they are needed because the church is incomplete without them?

      3) What can each of us do to connect with less involved or hurting church-goers? (Examples include: send a card, bake them cookies, offer a personal word of encouragement, call, or visit.) Ask participants to commit to doing something this week that will connect with and encourage someone who is hurting or isolated.

   e. Invite a volunteer to explain the circle of God's eternal love (p. 65). Guide them to discuss the circle and ask how its lessons apply to the church. Then ask participants how they would explain the importance of the church to someone who claims to be a believer but is not involved with church.

f. Ask participants to explain what it means to serve Christ in all aspects of their lives. Challenge them to consider what areas of their lives are not currently submitted to His service.

g. Ask, Do you believe you are ready for the return of Christ? Why or why not? Ask what they remember most about Peter's example of readiness.

4. Present your pre-selected service project idea. Tell the group you'd like to do something that could be incorporated into their group time as a way of experiencing the joy of service. Ask them to bring a canned food item for your church's food pantry, a baby item for your local Crisis Pregnancy center, or a donation to a local homeless center to next week's meeting. Or, you may choose to suggest that everyone stay a few minutes after your next session to tidy up the church or to weed the landscaping.

5. Divide participants into groups of three and ask each group to make an acrostic for the word church using some of the attributes seen in the portrait of the bride we studied in days 3–5. Give each group a blank piece of paper. After allowing 2–3 minutes work time, ask participants to share their results with the entire group. Examples include: C–consecrated or committed; H–holy or honorable; U–united or unblemished; R–radiant or ready; C–called or community; H–humble or happy.

6. Explain that one of the primary ways God empowers us for His service is through our spiritual gifts. Distribute copies of the Spiritual Gifts Review (see p. 152). Before participants begin writing, have a volunteer read 1 Corinthians 12:12-31 and Romans 12:3-8 (invite participants to follow along in their Bibles). Then ask participants to fill out their tests. After allowing 2–3 minutes work time, ask for the correct answers (F,T,T,T).

7. Invite participants to share their most significant insights from this week's study. Guide them to consider how their new understanding will change their actions.

8. Have each participant exchange her phone number with the classmate to her left. Ask the women to call one other during the week to offer encouragement and to get to know each other better.

9. Close in prayer. Thank God for giving believers lives with purpose and for the power to participate in divine partnership with Him. Praise God for allowing believers to grow in relationship with Him, and ask Him to encourage participants in a special way this week as they continue their journey to maturity. Ask God to give them strength and discipline as they continue in study.

10. Challenge participants to complete week 4's homework before the next session.

11. If applicable, remind participants to bring their donation item to next week's meeting.

After the Session

1. Take time to reflect on this session. Where do you see God working in the lives of group participants?

2. Commit to praying for each participant this week.

Session Four: Ornaments of Grace
Before the Session

1. Complete week 4's material. Use a highlighter to set off facts and insights that are especially meaningful to you. Be prepared to share your favorites with the group.

2. When you complete your week 4 homework, read through the list of discussion starters offered for this week's group session. Since you will not have time to do all of the suggested options, go ahead and circle 2 to 4 that you think your group might find valuable.

3. Ask God to reveal Himself to each participant in a very personal way this week. Ask the Holy Spirit to open participants' minds to better understand His plan for the church as she prepares for Christ's return.

4. Don't forget to purchase your item for the service project. If applicable, decorate a collection box or basket to receive project donations. You may want to consider making the service basket a permanent fixture in your women's ministry department–a reminder that attendants should always be busily devoted to meeting the church's needs.

5. Prepare a journal page for participants. Type *Journal* across the top of a standard size sheet of paper. List the four ornaments of grace and the thread of prayer down the right hand side, leaving a space for participants to record their experiences beside each. Make copies on brightly-colored paper for participants.

6. Obtain two blank sheets of paper for each participant and five posters or tear sheets for a group activity.

7. Provide colored yarn or clear, elastic line and enough of four different colored beads so each participant can make a bracelet representing the church's orna-

ments of grace. You'll also want to obtain enough clear colored beads for each participant to be able to fill in the remaining space of her bracelet. Cut the yarn or line into 11–12 inch strips, allowing plenty of room for wrists of all sizes as well as a tying tail. Don't forget you'll need scissors to trim the ends.

8. Select a CD or tape of praise music. Find songs about grace: "Amazing Grace," "Grace Greater Than Our Sin," "Your Grace Is Enough," "I Know Not Why God's Wondrous Grace," and "I Could Sing of Your Love Forever." Obtain a CD or tape player.

9. Arrive early and prepare your room for group session. Display the donation box or basket in a prominent place by the door.

During the Session (1 hour)

1. Welcome arriving participants. Warmly thank each person who brings an item for the service project.

2. Promptly begin the session with a time of praise and worship. Sing or listen to songs about grace.

3. Read 2 Corinthians 9:8 aloud. Pray, thanking God for His glorious grace and asking Him to make all grace abound through the church's ornaments.

4. Begin with some of these discussion starters:

   a. Remind the group of the meaning of *adorning*, *"to put in order, arrange, make ready, prepare."* Ask participants, Is our church today consciously (intentionally) preparing for Christ's return? Then invite participants to share some areas where they feel the church needs to do some rearranging to prepare for the return of Christ. Remind them to be kind and uplifting.

   b. Involve participants in a discussion of day 1's explanation of the differences between inner and outer adornments. Encourage participants to share their answers to the questions on page 72.

   c. Involve participants in a discussion of spiritual maturity. Ask, *What activities are important to our spiritual growth?* (For example: worship, prayer, Bible study, serving in our spiritual giftedness, and personal evangelism.) Guide them toward a commitment to more consistently practice these spiritual disciplines. Challenge them to focus on their personal spiritual development during the next week, taking note of signs of developing maturity. Ask them to be prepared to share examples and insights during your next meeting.

   d. Enlist a volunteer to read Jeremiah 2:32. Discuss what this verse reveals about the importance of wedding ornaments to a Jewish bride. Follow up by asking participants to consider whether or not the church today has lost sight of the value of her divine ornaments of grace. Ask them to explain their answers.

   e. Ask a volunteer to share how the infant church knew to focus on worship, instruction, fellowship, and evangelism. Then ask participants to explain why it's so important that none of the ornaments are neglected. Have them brainstorm ways they can take individual responsibility for making sure they are not.

   f. Invite participants to share examples of how they've been transformed by genuine worship. Ask how they can know when worship is real.

5. Write the word *grace* on the board or tear sheet. Ask participants to describe what the church would be like without the grace of God.

6. Divide participants into five groups. Assign each of four groups one of the ornaments of grace and the fifth group the thread of prayer. Ask them to explain how their assigned subject prepares us for Christ's return. After allowing 6–8 minutes of work time, ask each group to share their conclusions.

7. Write the word *fellowship* on the board or tear sheet. Then give each group a marker and tear sheet or poster board. Ask each group to make a simple drawing that expresses what fellowship means. After they have completed their drawings, give volunteers a chance to share their pictures with the class.

8. Ask each participant to think about her own personal salvation experience and what God has done in her life since that time. Give all participants a blank sheet of paper and ask them to write the story of their relationship with Christ. Encourage each participant to share her story with someone who does not know Christ before your next meeting.

9. Give each participant a piece of colored yarn or clear line and one of each of the four different colored beads. Then give each woman enough clear filler beads for each person in the class. Have participants work together to decide which color bead will represent which ornament of grace. Ideally, they should be in agreement on the color. Remind them that the yarn represents the thread of unceasing prayer.

Ask participants to "weave" the thread of prayer through each ornament of grace: worship, instruction, fellowship, and evangelism. Then ask them to collect one clear bead from each of the other participants. This will help remind them that Christ's bride is the collective church, working together to prepare for His return. Then lead participants to assist each other in tying the bracelets on. Suggest that participants wear the bracelets throughout the week as a reminder of the call to join together to prepare for Christ's coming.

10. Invite participants to share their most significant insights from this week's study. Look for indications that participants are learning to connect new insights with changed behavior. Affirm those who are beginning to do this without being prompted. Remind the group that translating insight into action is an important step in the process of personal transformation.

11. Pass out the journal pages you prepared. Explain that to fulfill God's purpose we must see the church as He sees her. Say, This week we'll seek to see our church with fresh eyes. Ask group participants to look for opportunities to observe each of the ornaments of grace in action as well as the thread of prayer binding them together. Invite them to record their experiences on the journal page, including a brief description of their experiences and how they each contributed to the preparation of Christ's bride.

12. Close the session with prayer, praising and thanking God for His marvelous grace. Thank God for all the blessings of community. Pray He will open eyes to see the bride of Christ's ornaments of grace more clearly and to encourage her attendants to be more actively involved in preparation.

13. Congratulate participants on their faithfulness to the homework assignments. Encourage them to press on as you enter the last few weeks of study.

After the Session

1. Take a few moments to reflect on this session.
2. Consider sending participants an invitation for coffee. Give each woman a call or e-mail, asking her to join you for a time of mid-week fellowship at a local coffee house, tearoom, or lunch stop. Use this time to get to know group members on a more personal level. Encourage group members to interact with each other.

Session Five: Messages From the Bridegroom
Before the Session

1. Complete week 5's material. Highlight the facts and insights that are especially meaningful to you. Be prepared to share your favorites with the group.
2. When you complete your week 5 homework, read through the list of discussion starters offered for this week's group session. Since you will not have time to do all of the suggested options, go ahead and circle 2 to 4 that you think might benefit your group.
3. Don't forget to fill out and be prepared to share the Journal page assigned during last week's meeting.
4. If you assigned the spiritual maturity exercise last week, ask volunteers to share their experiences. Be prepared to share your own insights.
5. Pray for each group member. Ask Christ to tune ears, open minds, and soften hearts to the important messages He has for His bride.
6. Arrive early and prepare the room for the small-group session.

During the Session (1 hour)

1. Welcome participants as they arrive.
2. Begin with prayer, asking God to prepare hearts for the session.
3. Ask a volunteer to share the results of last week's journal assignment. Give the opportunity for others to share as well.
4. Begin discussion with several of these starters:
   a. Have the group list the four messages revealed in Christ's formation of the church discussed in day one. Write each message on the board or tear sheet. Follow up by asking participants to share which of the messages they found most significant for the church today and why.
   b. Ask a volunteer to explain the symbolism of the individual lamp holders and lampstand mentioned in day 1. Encourage participants to evaluate their own lives. Ask, Are you giving proper attention to both your personal and community responsibilities in preparing for Christ's return? Brainstorm ways believers can remain more balanced in both areas of responsibility.
   c. Ask a volunteer to share 3 signs of a healthy love relationship. You may ask, How can you tell that a married couple is truly in love? Then

invite participants to list some signs of a church's healthy love relationship with Christ.

   d. Involve participants in a discussion contrasting the busyness of religious activity with the active lifestyle of true ministry.

   e. Ask how participants can help to protect the church against false teaching.

   f. Ask, What are some signs of a prideful church? Guide participants in a discussion of the dangers of a prideful church. Ask them how a church can rid itself of pride.

5. Divide participants into two groups. Ask group one to read 1 John 4:1-3 and describe one biblical test to detect false teaching. Ask group two to read Colossians 2:6-8 and develop a strategy for protecting oneself from false teaching. Allow time for each group to report.

6. Divide participants into five groups. Assign each group one of this week's daily lessons. Ask each group to prepare a brief summary of the bridegroom's messages from that day's lesson and to explain how it relates to the church today. After allowing 5–7 minutes work time, ask each group to share their report.

7. Bring the groups back together as a class. Work as a group to draft a love note back to Christ, responding to the admonitions and encouragements of His messages you studied this week. The goal is to express your love for and devotion to Him. You may want to start by brainstorming a list of things to include on a poster or tear sheet. Consider making a copy of the final draft for each participant.

8. Invite participants to share their most significant insight from this week's study. Encourage them to share what they will do differently based on any new understandings they've gained.

9. Divide the class into pairs. Ask each participant to share one prayer request with her partner concerning the ornament of grace with which she most struggles and then pray about it with her partner.

10. Close in prayer, thanking God for these important messages from His Word. Ask the Holy Spirit to continually remind you of these words as you prepare for Christ's return.

11. Challenge participants to complete before the last session week 6's homework and any other homework they may not have finished.

After the Session

1. Take a few moments to reflect on this session. Consider what spiritual or mental preparations you need to make for the final session. Make a note on the unit page of week 6.

2. Consider how to pray for each participant this week as the study comes to a close.

Session Six: The Bridegroom's Return
Before the Session

1. Complete week 6's material. Highlight facts and insights that are especially meaningful to you. Be prepared to share your favorites with the group.

2. When you complete your week 6 homework, read through the list of discussion starters offered for this week's group session. Since you will not have time to do all of the suggested options, go ahead and circle 2 to 4 that you think may benefit your group.

3. Specifically pray that all participants will experience a glimpse of the joy set before them during this week's study. Ask that God to prepare them to continue the transformation process after this study concludes.

4. Select a CD or tape of praise music that focuses on the return of Christ. (Consider songs like, "I Know My Redeemer Lives," "The Midnight Cry," "We Will Dance," or "I Can Only Imagine"). Obtain a CD player or tape player.

5. Bake or purchase a small, white wedding cake as well as some mints, mixed nuts, and punch. Prepare to decorate the classroom for a wedding shower. Consider enlisting the help of a few class participants to help make the celebration a success.

6. Type or print Revelation 19:6-9 and make copies for each participant.

7. Copy on colored card stock *My Commitment to Steadfast Devotion* for each participant (see p. 153).

8. Locate your list of reasons participants gave for taking this study (intro session).

9. Write with a marker on a poster or tear sheet the question, "Where do I go from here?"

10. Arrive early and prepare the room for your group session. Don't forget the food! Place the copies of Revelation 19:6-9 on each chair.

During the Session (1 hour)

1. Welcome participants as they arrive.

2. Begin the session promptly with praise and worship. Sing or listen to songs about the return of Christ.

3. Ask a volunteer to recite from memory or to read from her Bible John 14:1-3. Pray, thanking God that Christ will return to claim His Bride. Ask Him to help participants have unwavering faith in the certainty of Christ's return. Pray your church's believers will never lose sight of the joy set before them as they diligently prepare for His coming.

4. Begin with several of these discussion starters:
   a. Involve participants in a discussion of the importance of being certain that Christ will return.
   b. Ask participants to finish this statement: "You know you are longing for the return of Christ when …". Then ask the group to consider ways they can keep the certainty of Christ's return at the forefront of their thoughts and actions. List ideas on the board or tear sheet.
   c. Invite a volunteer to explain why knowing what we are to do until Jesus returns (our purpose) is more valuable than knowing when He will return. Ask, How can we remain focused on what we are called to do rather than being distracted by the exact timing of Christ's return? Challenge participants to cite verses that support their ideas.
   d. Ask a volunteer or have the group work together to develop a time line of the events that will occur when Christ returns according to 1 Thessalonians 4:14-17 and 1 Corinthians 15:35-44. Write the time line on a board or tear sheet.
   e. Ask group participants why it's important that they persevere in their preparations for the return of Christ. Invite a volunteer to share four things believers can do to persevere as they prepare for the divine bridegroom's return (pp. 136-138).

5. Review the three phases of the Jewish marriage experience using the ABC acronym. Write the name of each phase on the board or tear sheet. Divide participants into three groups, assigning each group one of the phases. Allow the groups 2–3 minutes work time before asking them to report on the spiritual realities reflected in their assigned phase.

6. Remind participants of my comments on page 132.
"Like many of you, I've been discouraged at times and wanted to give up on preparing and investing in the church. I often feel incapable of giving Christ's bride the attention and time she needs to prepare. But when this happens I remind myself that I'm depending on my own efforts instead of trusting God's miraculous power."

Ask, Has anyone else ever had similar feelings? Share ways believers can encourage one another to persevere through disappointment and discouragement. If appropriate, stop and pray about the feelings shared.

7. Ask a volunteer to read this excerpt from *Under the Wedding Canopy: Love and Marriage in Judaism.*
"One can say that a Jewish wedding ceremony is like a replay of Jewish history and Jewish teaching. The new couple is connected to ancient days to Patriarchs and Matriarchs, to hope and prayer. When the couple steps away from the wedding canopy, now married and proclaiming to the world that they are husband and wife, they have established themselves as a new link in the long chain of Jewish history."[2]

Involve participants in a discussion of how their commitment to Christ is another link in the chain leading to Christ's return. Ask how their commitment levels to Christ affect future generations.

8. Invite participants to share their most significant insights from this journey. Remind them of the personal assessment exercise from week 1. Encourage participants to share testimonies of how their lives have been changed through this journey. Praise God for all He has accomplished during your time together!

9. Remind the group of reasons they gave for taking this study. Read the list you compiled after the introductory session. Involve participants in a discussion evaluating both their original reasons for taking the study and the results they have experienced.

10. Point out the question on the board or tear sheet, "Where do I go from here?" Ask participants to think carefully about that question and then respond.

11. Commend participants for their commitment to study God's Word. Tell them this study may be over but the lessons continue. Challenge participants to allow God to help them put what they have learned into practice. Remind them that what they do matters!

12. Explain that one way believers can remember their commitment to Christ is to put what they learn to practice; to keep learning and to keep attending. Distribute copies of the *My Commitment of Steadfast Devotion* card. Provide time for each participant to read the card. Ask a volunteer to pray before participants consider making this important commitment. Then invite them to sign and date the card. Encour-

age them to keep the card where they will see it (on a bathroom mirror, the refrigerator, in their Bibles, or taped to the dashboard of their cars).

13. Ask participants to continue offering ongoing encouragement and accountability for one another now that the class is over. Suggest that everyone meet again in one month in a home, a favorite lunch spot, or tea room. Try to schedule a "bridesmaid luncheon" where you'll be able to share testimonies of what God will do in your hearts and lives over the next weeks.

14. Read Revelation 19:6-9 as a group from the paper you prepared so that everyone is reading from the same translation.

15. Close in prayer. Thank the Lord for your time together and for allowing you to be a part of His awesome plan. Ask God to help participants attend Christ's bride with steadfast devotion. Pray that they will continue to learn and grow, allowing God to continue the process of our transformation.

16. End with a time a celebration. Turn up the praise music. Serve the wedding cake, punch, and other treats. You may even choose to throw confetti, but be sure to clean it up afterwards if you do!

After the Session

1. Write a note of affirmation and encouragement to each group participant. Thank them for sharing their lives with you during these past weeks. Commit to continue to pray for them as the Lord leads. Invite them to contact you with specific prayer needs. Encourage them to keep learning from God and to continue allowing Him to change their behavior.

2. Follow up on any special needs.

3. Follow through on plans for ongoing encouragement to the study participants.

Praise God for all He has done and thank Him for the opportunity to be a part of this journey.

Spiritual Gifts Review

Mark the following statements True ("T") or False ("F").

_____ All believers have the same gifts

_____ All gifts are equally valuable

_____ No believer has all the gifts

_____ Each gift has the same function

My Commitment of Steadfast Devotion

I joyfully accept the honor of attending Christ and His bride with steadfast devotion. Relying on God's wisdom and strength, I commit to seeing the church as Christ sees her and acting toward her as He would act.

I will allow God to continue the process of my personal transformation as I wholeheartedly join with other believers in the preparations for Christ's return.

I will strive to keep the joy of Christ's return ever before me and seek to encourage others to do so.

Signed _Joy Turner_ Today's date _7/25/2011_

KINGDOM CALENDAR

Arrangement Phase of Relationship between Christ and His church

- God chose Christ's bride
- Christ paid the bride price
- Christ and His church covenant to remain sanctified
- New covenant sealed by the Holy Spirit

Betrothal Phase of Relationship between Christ and His church

- The church is called to prepare for Christ's return
- Christ works with His Father to prepare
- The church is prepared as believers join together with God
- Individual believers attend the bride of Christ through the Holy Spirit

Celebration Phase of Relationship between Christ and His church

- God, the Father, decides everything is ready
- God sends Christ to claim His bride
- The trumpet [shofar] will sound
- The divine wedding celebration begins

Creation	Birth of Christ	Ascension of Christ	Pentecost	God Determines Time	Return of Christ	Wedding of The Lamb

The ABC's of Salvation

Some people think a personal relationship with God is something only theologians can comprehend. Actually, God's plan of salvation is simple enough for everyone to understand. Here are the ABC's of salvation.

Admit

Admit to God that you are a sinner. All persons need salvation. Each of us has a problem the Bible calls sin. Sin is a refusal to acknowledge God's authority over our lives. Everyone who does not live a life of perfect obedience to the Lord is guilty of sin. "For all have sinned and fall short of the glory of God" (Romans 3:23). Since none of us is perfect, all of us are sinners (Romans 3:10-18).

The result of sin is spiritual death (Romans 6:23). Spiritual death means eternal separation from God. By God's perfect standard we are guilty of sin and therefore subject to the punishment for sin, which is separation from God. Admitting that you are a sinner and separated from God is the first step of repentance, which is turning from sin and self and turning toward God.

Believe

Believe in Jesus Christ as God's Son and receive Jesus' gift of forgiveness from sin. God loves each of us. God offers us salvation. Although we have done nothing to deserve His love and salvation, God wants to save us. In the death of Jesus on the cross, God provided salvation for all who would repent of their sins and believe in Jesus. "For God loved the world in this way: He gave His one and only Son, so that everyone who believes in Him will not perish but have eternal life" (John 3:16).

If you would like to have salvation in Jesus Christ, sincerely pray a prayer like this one: "Dear God, I confess to You my sin and need for salvation. I turn away from my sin and place my faith in Jesus as my Savior and Lord. Amen."

Confess

Confess your faith in Jesus Christ as Savior and Lord to others. After you have received Jesus Christ into your life, share your decision with another person. Tell your Bible study group, your pastor, or a Christian friend about your decision. Following Christ's example, ask for baptism by immersion in your local church as a public expression of your faith. "If you confess with your mouth, 'Jesus is Lord,' and believe in your heart that God raised Him from the dead, you will be saved. With the heart one believes, resulting in righteousness, and with the mouth one confesses, resulting in salvation" (Romans 10:9-10).

Becoming a Christian is your first step on the lifelong road of spiritual growth and service God desires for you as you become actively involved in a local church.

Acknowledgments

Writing a book is no solo effort. Many people worked behind the scenes to make this study possible. I'd like to extend thanks to:

My family who made great sacrifices during this time of writing. I want to express special appreciation to my husband, Roger. His unfailing love and devotion is a living example of Christ's relationship with the Church. He read and reread each draft, offering valuable suggestions. Without his support and encouragement I would never have completed this journey. Thanks to my two youngest children, Katie and Taylor, for their love and support. They both gave up some "Mom time" and took on a few extra chores. To my oldest daughter, Amber, and son-in-law, Keith, for their love and encouragement. To my parents, Jim and Iris Bell, for always believing in me. I'm blessed with a loving, caring, and supportive family. I pray God will repay them for their many sacrifices.

My editorial team at LifeWay has played a vital role in refining the final product. Specifically, I am indebted to Dale for his unwavering support for this message, to Bethany for giving her whole heart to the manuscript and for remaining sensitive to my feelings as she helped me express myself more clearly, and to Joyce for gently challenging me to go further. To Jon for his vision for the beautiful cover and giving extra attention to my author photos. To Melissa for her wonderful art work on the cover and unit pages. They have each added something very special to this study, and I'm forever grateful.

My dear friend, Karen Finke, deserves special thanks. She played an important role in the early development of this study. I'm grateful for her help and our shared passion for this message. My life has been blessed by Karen's willingness to freely lend her gifts and her courage to follow God.

Thank you to my precious friend, Myra Martin, and the Attending the Bride of Christ prayer warriors for their steadfast love and prayer support. Under Myra's guidance, these amazing women of prayer from around the country faithfully prayed during each stage of this journey. Their tireless devotion has been an inspiration to me.

I'm so grateful to my friends, Chris and the LifeWay Women's Ministry Multipliers, for their enthusiasm and encouragement. I'm blessed to be a part of this team of talented and vision-driven women who transparently model steadfast devotion to Christ and His bride.

To the members of my home church in Worland, Wyoming for their prayers and words of affirmation. I'm greatly honored to serve the bride of Christ alongside them!

I am most grateful to God for trusting me with this opportunity and for providing the strength, guidance, and spiritual protection needed to complete it. May He receive all the glory!

Notes

_____

_____

_____

_____

_____

_____

_____

_____

_____

_____

_____

_____

_____

_____

_____

_____

_____

_____

Notes

Notes

_____

_____

_____

_____

_____

_____

_____

_____

_____

_____

_____

_____

_____

_____

_____

_____

_____

Two Ways to Earn Credit
for Studying LifeWay Christian Resources Material

CONTACT INFORMATION:
Christian Growth Study Plan
One LifeWay Plaza, MSN 117
Nashville, TN 37234
CGSP info line 1-800-968-5519
www.lifeway.com/CGSP
To order resources 1-800-485-2772

Christian Growth Study Plan resources are available for course credit for personal growth and church leadership training.

Courses are designed as plans for personal spiritual growth and for training current and future church leaders. To receive credit, complete the book, material, or activity. Respond to the learning activities or attend group sessions, when applicable, and show your work to your pastor, staff member, or church leader. Then go to *www.lifeway.com/CGSP*, or call the toll-free number for instructions for receiving credit and your certificate of completion.

For information about studies in the Christian Growth Study Plan, refer to the current catalog online at the CGSP Web address. This program and certificate are free LifeWay services to you.

Need a CEU?

CONTACT INFORMATION:
CEU Coordinator
One LifeWay Plaza, MSN 150
Nashville, TN 37234
Info line 1-800-968-5519
www.lifeway.com/CEU

Receive Continuing Education Units (CEUs) when you complete group Bible studies by your favorite LifeWay authors.

Some studies are approved by the Association of Christian Schools International (ACSI) for CEU credits. Do you need to renew your Christian school teaching certificate? Gather a group of teachers or neighbors and complete one of the approved studies. Then go to *www.lifeway.com/CEU* to submit a request form or to find a list of ACSI-approved LifeWay studies and conferences. Book studies must be completed in a group setting. Online courses approved for ACSI credit are also noted on the course list. The administrative cost of each CEU certificate is only $10 per course.